PAINTING &
WALLPAPERING

Created and designed
by the editorial staff
of ORTHO Books

Project Editor	Sally W. Smith
Writer	Robert C. Yeager
Designer	Jacqueline Jones
Illustrator	Rik Olson
Photographer	Stephen Marley
Photographic Stylist	Sara Slavin

Ortho Books

Publisher
Robert L. Iacopi

Editorial Director
Min S. Yee

Managing Editors
Anne Coolman
Michael D. Smith

Photographic Director
Alan Copeland

System Managers
Chris Banks
Mark Zielinski

Senior Editor
Sally W. Smith

Editors
Jim Beley
Susan Lammers
Deni Stein

Production Manager
Laurie Sheldon

Photographers
Laurie A. Black
Richard A. Christman
Michael D. McKinley

System Assistant
William Yusavage

Photo Editors
Anne Dickson-Pederson
Pam Peirce

Production Editors
Alice E. Mace
Kate O'Keeffe

Production Assistant
Darcie S. Furlan

National Sales Manager
Garry P. Wellman

Sales Assistant
Susan B. Boyle

Operations/Distribution
William T. Pletcher

Operations Assistant
Donna M. White

Administrative Assistant
Georgiann Wright

Address all inquiries to
Ortho Books
Chevron Chemical Company
Consumer Products Division
Box 5047
San Ramon, CA 94583

Chevron Chemical Company
6001 Bollinger Canyon Road, San Ramon, CA 94583

Acknowledgments

Photographic Locations
Diane Saeks
San Francisco, CA

Nancy Adams
Chicago, IL

Designers
Page 4
Susan Gard, I.S.I.D.
Susan Gard Interiors
San Jose, CA

Page 7
Antonio F. Torrice
Just Between Friends
San Francisco, CA

Pages 9 and 20 (left)
Beverly Gilbert, Lucy Ledoux,
and Caron Weinstein
Designers Studio
Danville, CA 94526

Pages 10 and 13
Tony Pisacane
San Francisco, CA

Page 12
Marliese G. Jones, I.S.I.D.
Belmont, CA

Page 15, top
Scott C. Lamb, A.S.I.D.
San Francisco, CA

Page 15, bottom
Jayne Dranias
River Forest, IL

Page 16
John K. Wheatman, Dudley
Williams, Nancy C. Minard,
and Helen Reed Craddick
Cole-Wheatman, Inc.
San Francisco, CA

Page 19
Ilene Sanford
Ilene Sanford Interior Designs
San Francisco, CA

Page 20, right
Ron Smith, Bonnie Sue Smith,
and Joyce Ferrando
J. Hettinger Interiors &
Associates
Danville, CA

Page 21
Louise Barton Fisher, A.S.I.D.,
and Charlyne Brown,
Associate member, A.S.I.D.
Creekside Interiors
Lafayette, CA

Page 22
David Smith
Interior and Furniture Design
Sausalito, CA

Page 23, top
Arlene Semel
Arlene Semel & Associates
Chicago, IL

Page 23, bottom
Charles Taylor
Charles Taylor Interior Design
San Ramon, CA

Page 26
Jois
San Francisco, CA

Page 50
Designers Four
Walnut Creek, CA

Page 56
Cynthia Roberts
San Francisco, CA

Page 87
Marilyn Roy
Sassie Lassie Designs
Diablo, CA

Special Thanks to:
Camron-Stanford House
Dr. and Mrs. J. M. Davidson
Tony Pisacane
Cynthia and Jim Roberts
David and Pia Smith
Tony Torrice
Wallpapers, Inc.
Peggy and Geoffrey Tilleard

Additional Photography
Page 15, bottom
Photo Ideas, Inc.,
Chicago, IL

**Design and Technical
Consultants**
Bob Beckstrom
The Owner Builder Center
Berkeley, CA

Charles Crookston
San Francisco, CA

Joanne Day
The Day Studio-Workshop, Inc.
San Francisco, CA

Louise Barton Fisher, A.S.I.D.,
and Charlyne Brown,
Associate member, A.S.I.D.
Creekside Interiors
Lafayette, CA

Jerry Miller
J. Hettinger Interiors
Danville, CA

National Paint & Coatings
Association
Washington, D.C.

Rodney V. Reclus
San Francisco, CA

Robert T. Schmitz
San Francisco, CA

Virginia Soffa Viets
Quintessence
Walnut Creek, CA

Wallcovering Manufacturers
Association
Springfield, NJ

R. Scot Webster
San Francisco, CA

Editorial Assistance
Beverley DeWitt

**Copyediting and
Proofreading**
Editcetera
Berkeley, CA

Graphic Design Assistant
Mary Lynne Barbis

Illustration Assistants
Marilyn Hill
Amy Pertschuk

Typesetting
CBM Type
Sunnyvale, CA

Color Separation
Color Tech
Redwood City, CA

Front Cover

Paint and wallpaper set the style
and tone of a room. Laura
Ashley's delicate "Campion" in
lavender-blue will be com-
plemented by mixed-to-match
wall paint, white trim paint, and
natural wood floors. Photograph
by Michael Lamotte.

Page 1

Author Robert C. Yeager, a
San Francisco writer, recently
completed restoring a 70-
year-old home.

Back Cover

Clockwise from top left:
Wallpaper and coordinating paint
in a breakfast room; ceiling
border and companion drapes in
a child's room; padded and
backtacked fabric trimmed with
gimp in a romantic bedroom; a
monochromatic color scheme in
a youngster's room.

PAINTING &
WALLPAPERING

DESIGNING WITH PAINT & WALLCOVERINGS

The photographs and guidelines
in this chapter explain basic design
elements that will help you get the effects you
want with paint and wallcoverings.
Use the shoppers' guide on page 25 to
make your final decisions.

From earliest times, those who could afford them hired artisans to create interiors that soothed the spirit and pleased the eye. Gradually, the art of interior decoration spread throughout society. Today, the design of interior space has become a recognized profession.

If you're a typical homeowner or apartment dweller, however, hiring a professional designer—to say nothing of outside painting and decorating contractors —remains a luxury. Most of us must rely on our own skills as interior designer, painter, and wallcovering hanger. This book is designed to help. Chapter 2 covers everything you need to know about painting, including special treatments such as painting with glazes and stenciling. Chapter 3 supplies complete information on wallcoverings, including fabric. But first, let this chapter guide you in planning your own interior design.

Design

How can you use paint and/or wallcovering to greatest advantage in your particular surroundings? What considerations influence the choice between paint and wallpaper? How can you select the right color paint or the appropriate wallcovering pattern? To choose a color and pattern scheme you'll be able to live with contentedly, you should be familiar with the elements of design discussed on the following pages: light—the effect of artificial and natural light on your design; continuity —the sense of consistency within and between your

This dining area reflects skillful use of design principles. Paint, wallpaper, and fabric combine in an appealing but restrained interplay of complement and contrast. A dark paint, related to the paper's background color, helps lower the apparent ceiling height. The chair rail smooths the transition between different wall colors and materials.

rooms; space—the scale of a room as it is affected by wall treatments; contrast—the interplay of opposites; texture —the real or apparent "feelability" of wall surfaces. Before you start on those subjects, however, it may be worthwhile to review one of the most basic lessons in interior design: the focal point wall.

The focal point wall. The focal point wall is the first wall you see when you enter the room. As you read the following pages, think about the effect you wish to achieve on the focal point wall. It will make your strongest design statement and thus set the tone for the rest of the room.

In some instances, such as a square room with an off-center doorway, the focal point occurs in a corner, and you may safely accent either or both walls to its sides. When in doubt, remember this rule: the focal point (wall or corner) is the first prominent feature you see when approaching from the room's commonly used entryway.

Being yourself. The most important interior design principle is the familiar maxim: know yourself. What colors and patterns do you like and feel comfortable with? Analyze your taste by finding some rooms—in your own or a friend's home or in photographs—that please you. Try to identify their common stylistic points: a particular type of architecture, a family of colors, certain kinds of furniture, and so on. Look for details such as molding and hardware. What window style, quantity of light, and window treatment go with your favorites? The answers to these questions can help define your personal style. If you're still uncertain about your taste, try this easy exercise. Gather five or six household or clothing items whose colors and patterns please you. Place them on a plain surface such as a tabletop and move them around until you find a combination you like. Now try to analyze the arrangement. What color or pattern dominates? Do you favor subdued, monochromatic schemes or more daring combinations? What kinds of patterns do you prefer? The answers should lead you to an accurate portrait of your own color and pattern comfort zone. Study the design principles on the following pages with your color and pattern style in mind.

DESIGN: COLOR

Color is to the eye what music is to the ear. Color can affect the size of a room, its mood, even its temperature. To work with color effectively, you need to understand its three major variables, discussed below.

Light and dark. As a rule, light colors open or enlarge a room, and dark colors close it in, shrinking its apparent proportions. But there is more than that to the phenomenon of light and dark. The lightest color, for instance, isn't white; yellow emits more light. Nor is white the easiest color choice you can make. Because of its wide range of tints and shades, white is one of the most difficult colors to choose accurately. And dark paint, used with dramatic lighting or in combination with light-colored walls, can actually make a room look larger than it would if all surfaces had been painted a single light color. For more information on color and space, see page 14.

Warm and cool. Many paint manufacturers and interior designers divide the thousands of shades of color into just two groups, warm and cool. Cool colors generally have blue or green undertones; warm colors generally have red or yellow undertones. The terms *warm* and *cool* relate to the "feeling" of rooms painted in those colors; you can make a room seem friendly and welcoming by giving it a warm color scheme. You can also bring interest to a room by contrasting the warmth or coolness of the wall with your room's daylight exposure; see page 11 for an explanation of this technique.

Bright and intense. Colors also possess qualities of brightness and intensity. In general, a bright color *reflects* light, an intense color *reacts with* light. An intense color such as chartreuse vibrates, especially when placed against a contrasting warm or cool shade. Sunny yellow may sparkle, but it is nonetheless only a bright hue, not an intense one. Many manufacturers today label especially intense paints "accent" colors. Both bright and intense colors can be so strong that you should use them with restraint, perhaps on only one wall. But such colors can be very helpful—as a livening touch painted on trim, for instance, or in providing a focal point wall in a room with many different elements.

Dominant Color

Just as every room possesses a focal point wall, so it has a dominant color, which you must take into account when selecting paint and wallcoverings. It is usually determined by the largest single element of color in a room —existing floor coverings, drapes, or, perhaps, a king-size bedspread. The dominant color will point to your color scheme; once you've identified it, you'll choose other colors to harmonize with it.

The Color Wheel

The color wheel is a way of representing the natural prism, based on the three primary colors—red, blue, and yellow—and the colors they form when combined. Thus green is a mix of blue and yellow; aqua is a bluish green and chartreuse is a yellow-green. In its simplest form, as shown at right, the wheel contains the 12 base colors, but it can be expanded to show any number of modulations between the three primary colors.

The color wheel can help you identify the components of a color. In interior decorating, true colors—the hues you see in the wheel—are seldom used except as accents, because their purity makes them too intense for large areas. Instead, tints (base colors lightened by whites) and shades (base colors deepened by black) are usually employed. The color bar below right shows the gradations of one color from a light tint through a dark shade. Such a grouping creates a monochromatic color scheme, an example of which is shown on the facing page. Another pleasing way to combine colors is to select tints or shades of complementary colors—which lie directly opposite one another on the color wheel —and then make additions from the same families. In the picture on page 4, the wall and ceiling colors are related tones with the same orange undertone, and the accent color is a pale tint of orange's complement, blue. In selecting a color scheme, confine your choices to the dominant color plus two or three others; few rooms can take more than four colors.

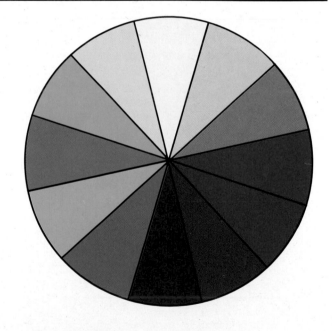

How Color Can Solve Problems

Color can help you emphasize or diminish the architectural features of your room. For example, painting trim the same color as the walls can make the trim virtually disappear. That might be desirable if your woodwork isn't particularly attractive, or if your room is small: contrasting trim would emphasize the narrow confines of the room. Similarly, you could paint a built-in cabinet that juts out into the room the same shade as the walls to blend it into its surroundings, or you could paint it a contrasting color to point up its style, create a focal point, or add interest to the room.

And color can improve the continuity of your living space, by pulling disparate elements, even separate rooms, into a more pleasing whole. (The importance of continuity in design is discussed in greater detail on pages 12–13.) For example, designers often use wallpaper as a "bridge" to tie together a medley of colors. Say you're stuck with bathroom fixtures in an unappealing color. Painting or papering as if they weren't there will only make the objects more prominent; their color will stand out like an accent color against the contrasting background. The solution? Choose a wallpaper pattern containing a small amount of the offending color and a larger quantity of a color you'd prefer. The wallpaper will bridge the color gap and blend your fixtures into a more harmonious whole.

A powerful dose of color may be just right for a child. Several tones of one primary, blue, form this monochromatic scheme, with accents of the other two primaries, red and yellow, plus a little green. To balance the room's intensity, the designer has introduced contrasting white trim and natural wood.

DESIGN: PATTERN

Wallcoverings come in a wide variety of designs and materials, including hand-screened papers, all-vinyl coverings, foil, flocked designs, woven fabrics, sheeting, and even "natural" materials like cork, pasted straw, and leaves. Nearly all coverings possess their own *pattern*, but the term is most commonly used to describe printed designs on paper. Pattern shares equal billing with color as a major design element in any room; it has the same capability to set a mood, create interest, or unify a room. Pattern on paper can often be combined with pattern on fabric. Manufacturers offer a wide selection of pattern-coordinated papers and fabrics, and you can come up with your own combinations as well.

How to Look at Pattern

You'll find it hard to "see" a pattern simply by looking at a sample in a book. The best way to appreciate a pattern is to see it over a wide expanse of wall. A photograph of a papered room will help you judge a pattern. If all you can work with is samples, however, try to get a loose one or at least temporarily borrow the book—most dealers are quite willing to loan them. Place the sample where you plan to hang the paper. Stand back and take a careful look at how the pattern affects the room. Apart from the suitability of its color or scale (see below), try to imagine the overall impact of the design repeated across the wall. When seen at a distance, the pattern may create an additional effect, such as diagonal stripes. The paper pictured on the opposite page, for instance, has a subtle pattern-within-a-pattern of large squares that would not be apparent in a small sample. Often the best way to analyze the effect of pattern is to squint your eyes so the unimportant details drop away, revealing the underlying structure of the design.

Background Color

Every wallpaper has a background color. Dark backgrounds can overpower a room, so most are light, but you may well desire a strong background for contrast or drama or just a potent punch of color. You can speed up your wallcovering decision by deciding fairly early whether you want a strong background; flipping the page corners of sample books will allow you to eliminate designs with the wrong color background. If you prefer a dark background color, make certain your room is well lighted, whether from natural, incandescent, or reflected sources (see page 11 for a discussion of light). Without good lighting, the room will seem too dark and the paper itself will not stand out clearly.

Texture and Unity

Pattern can be employed to create an effect of texture on your walls or, like color, to unify a room. Texture, of course, can be achieved with a wallcovering like grasscloth or burlap (see page 18 for a discussion of texture), but such coverings can be expensive. You can also create texture with pattern, especially tightly printed, redundant designs. Again, though, be forewarned: it may be difficult to see the texture by looking at the small sections of paper in a sample book.

To unify a room with a number of disparate elements—a hallway with many doors or a room with dormers or other irregularities, perhaps—you'll want a uniform wallcovering. Small patterns are especially effective in such cases. For more information on unity, see "Continuity Within Rooms" on page 12.

Pattern alone can impart a strong tactile impression, lending a wallcovering the "feelability" usually associated with actual textures such as cork or grasscloth (see page 18). In the bedroom on the opposite page, close-set diagonal lines give the illusion of a finely scored surface that provides an effective complement to the flat finish painted above it.

Pattern and Scale

Large-scale patterns are characterized by widely separated big design motifs and backgrounds with plenty of open space. Small-scale patterns feature little motifs with closely spaced repeats. In general, large-scale motifs belong in large rooms, small-scale in small rooms. A disproportionate pattern can make a room unattractive, even uncomfortable. But with careful judgment, you can experiment with scale. A small entry hall may look elegant and grand with one wall covered in a large-scale pattern. A small-scale design can work in a large room if it is combined with borders or set into panels edged with molding.

Small-scale pattern

Large-scale pattern

DESIGN: LIGHT

The effect of different lighting conditions can be seen in the two photographs above. This dining room is painted two subtly different shades of soft pink. The top photograph shows the room in natural light, which brings out the pink tones in the color. At night, in artificial light, the gray tones of the paint predominate.

Thinking About Light

As your own interior decorator, you should be aware that light is never neutral. Apart from the role daylight plays in the choice between warm and cool color schemes, light itself is an important element in your room. Because colors change under different lighting conditions, any color selection should be made in the light under which it will primarily be viewed. You'll also need to consider the furnishings and the amount of light in the room. Light will have an effect on each design decision you make.

Light sources. Is the light in your room direct or reflected? Is it natural, fluorescent, or incandescent? Each type will have a different effect on the colors you choose. Fluorescent lights have pink or blue undertones; incandescent light and sunlight have a yellow cast. Subtle as they are, such tones can influence almost any neutral color. Reflected light carries the memory of its parent surface. For example, if you put up blue curtains or paint a ceiling blue, white paint on the walls will seem to be a blue white; if, instead, you use red at the windows, the wall color will appear to have a pink cast.

Furnishings and light. In general, with fabrics as with wall finishes, flat surfaces absorb light and shiny surfaces reflect it. So a deep cordovan leather sofa in the living room or a dark cotton bedspread in the bedroom will soak up light. If you're choosing a wall finish to maximize the light in the room, you wouldn't want to undercut your effort with an absorbent fabric. Instead you might choose a shiny chintz for the sofa, or a satin bedspread. You can, of course, deliberately vary the fabrics in a room to create contrast; a glossy paint might be paired with a flat fabric, or a matte wall finish with a reflective one.

Amount of light. Most of us prefer a well-lighted room, but there are occasions when too much light spoils a good thing. Careful contrast of light and dark can heighten a room's drama and appeal. The combination of low artificial lighting and warm-toned walls can create an intimate mood; flooding such a room with natural light will spoil the effect. On the other hand, be realistic. A room with a large skylight is not going to look cozy even if you do paint the walls a rich, dark color. If a room is dominated by abundant sunlight, match it with light, airy colors and patterns to create a playful, happy feeling. Working with the light in your room, not against it, will produce the most pleasing result.

Light and Exposure

What does solar exposure have to do with painting and wallcovering? A great deal, as it turns out. If your home happens to be a small apartment with a northern exposure, for example, you may well have only one or two walls with windows, and your light will be indirect daylight. If you choose dark colors and patterns, your taste and pocketbook better be ready for a lot of artificial light. Paint those same rooms in cool blues and lime greens and you'll get the shivers. In homes with eastern and southeastern exposures (morning sunlight) and rooms with western exposures (late-afternoon sunlight), you'll find those cool colors refreshing. Of course, you can take the lessons of light and exposure too far: bright yellow probably isn't the best color to paint a living room, even if it receives only minimal sunlight. You'll also want to take into account outside plants and vegetation and the time of day you use the room most frequently. Such caveats aside, however, the general point is still well taken: use warm colors in rooms with northern exposure, cooler tones in rooms with southern exposure. The illustration below shows one designer's recommendations.

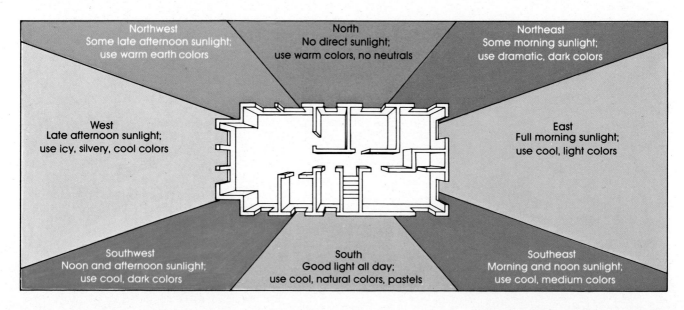

Northwest
Some late afternoon sunlight; use warm earth colors

North
No direct sunlight; use warm colors, no neutrals

Northeast
Some morning sunlight; use dramatic, dark colors

West
Late afternoon sunlight; use icy, silvery, cool colors

East
Full morning sunlight; use cool, light colors

Southwest
Noon and afternoon sunlight; use cool, dark colors

South
Good light all day; use cool, natural colors, pastels

Southeast
Morning and noon sunlight; use cool, medium colors

DESIGN: CONTINUITY

In interior design, continuity means consistency within rooms; from room to room; and, in rooms with large doors and windows, even with the outside environment. Continuity is achieved only when paint and wallcoverings display an underlying feeling of organization and unity, one that can tie together, say, cabinets and ceilings in the kitchen to a wallpaper visible in an adjoining dining room. Proper use of continuity can help disguise *dis*continuity—that is, inevitable awkward architectural details and spaces that can rob otherwise pleasant surroundings of their charm.

The First Thing You See
Stand in the open front door of your home, looking in. Which walls play on one another? You can always see one wall in front of another at some point—perhaps the living room against the dining room, or the dining room against the kitchen. Notice how dark walls recede, and light ones come forward. Do the colors or patterns harmonize (without being dull) or clash? Your answers should help in planning and choosing both paint and wallcoverings.

Continuity Between Rooms
Something's wrong if you're startled by a feeling of abrupt change when you move from one room to another. One way to produce a sense of cohesion is to choose paint and wallcoverings from related color and pattern families. For example, the wallcovering in a dressing area off a master bedroom might pick up a color or pattern from the bedroom drapes. Or companion papers of differing scales might tie together a family room and kitchen. Often, of course, a major continuity decision will be made for you in the form of preexisting carpet or other floor covering. If it extends through several rooms, it can help expand a small house or apartment. Whatever your situation, the key is maintaining a pleasing room-to-room flow, with special attention to the places where more than one room can be seen at once.

Continuity Within Rooms
As with unity between rooms, ensuring a sense of continuity within a given room means taking a close look wherever different surfaces juxtapose. Do brick or concrete walls butt against plaster or wood? Brick, for example, is often left unpainted, but in some instances its deep red color, irregular texture, and the strong horizontal-vertical crosshatch pattern created by mortar lines interrupt the continuity of a room.

Furnishings, especially drapes, can help make a cohesive room. You can repeat one fabric, or a pair of related ones, in different parts of the room, but you can also link fabric and wallcoverings. You might pick up a design element from drapes or upholstery and stencil it onto the walls, as in the bathroom at left, or use a motif from wallpaper as a design for hand-worked pillows or chair cushions.

Architectural features may break the lines of a room into a series of fragmented areas. A small-scale pattern can pull them together. Similarly, such architectural details as doors, windows, and ceiling moldings can interrupt the flow of an expanse of wall. Painting walls, doors, and trim all the same color can help blend and unify the irregularities.

The stenciling on the walls (left) duplicates the motif on the fabric used in this bathroom curtain, creating continuity and interest in a room that otherwise would be undistinguished. The freehand arrangement of the stencils requires an artistic eye; for an easier technique, see pages 52–53.

At right, gray leather furniture sets a color tone that links the two rooms. The pink of the room in the foreground and the blue of the farther room are grayed and softened to the same degree. Shared molding treatment and floor finish further unify the two rooms.

Continuity With the Outdoors

What's outside your home? If you've got large window areas shrouded in leafy shrubs, you're almost certain to get a green cast on your walls. If you have big picture windows that look out on a dramatic landscape, you'll want to take that into account as well.

Basically, to maintain continuity, your strategic choice is this: either screen off the outside environment with a heavy window covering, or bring it in to integrate those exterior elements with the colors and patterns you choose for the interior of your room. The eye-catching views through large picture windows, for example, would probably doom any attempt to draw attention to a contrasting interior color or pattern. So the best course might well be to pick up a color from the outside landscape—the light, tawny brown of a field, perhaps —and use that for your walls.

Continuity With Other Materials

Some manufacturers offer wallcoverings with matching fabrics to make it easy to tie together wallpaper, drapery, bedspreads, and other items. Companion papers, which allow the use of different but complementary scales, colors, and themes in separate but related rooms, are another help. These are easy ways of improving continuity, but they won't eliminate your need to be aware of architecture, the color of adjoining spaces, and other important details.

The keys to continuity are planning and judgment. Concentrate on the critical points—the places where wall and floor surfaces meet, where hallways and doors open into adjoining rooms. But don't overdo it. Continuity should never appear contrived. And it needs to be balanced with contrast—in scale, color, texture, and pattern—to make a room attractive.

DESIGN: SPACE

In the process of purchasing paint or wallcoverings, you're going to measure off your rooms to determine their perimeter, height, square footage, and so forth. That should tell you how high the area you're tackling is in terms of feet and inches, but it may not say much at all about how big it *feels*. That dimension is determined by esthetics, not tape measures.

What is space? What does it mean? A long hallway with a dark-painted door at the end *seems* shorter than a corridor of the same length ending in a light-colored door. Horizontal-striped wallpaper can make a rectangular room look longer if hung on the longest wall, wider if hung on an end, focal point wall. Shiny surfaces increase space, matte ones absorb and diminish it. As a concept, space is elusive, but worth understanding.

Color and Space

In general, lighter walls, ceilings, and floors push the boundaries of a room away, making it look larger. Dark finishes or strong, vibrating colors crowd in toward the viewer, bringing surfaces closer. That may be desirable if you want an intimate feeling, but if you prefer openness, opt for light walls and ceilings. If a surface seems too distant, color it dark; if it seems too close, color it light. For the same reasons, painting a chair rail with a dark, contrasting enamel will define the perimeter of a room. Using a color that matches that of the wall will help open the room up. Remember, too, that light itself—whether from the sun or artificial sources—adds to space, which explains why reflective coatings and coverings expand the sense of space.

With color and space, however, as in most areas of design, there are few hard and fast rules. For example, dark colors may on occasion be used to *increase* perceived space. In a small room with windows on a single wall, painting that focal point wall with a dark color while using a light color on the other surfaces will result in a more open "look" than would finishing all four walls and the ceiling in a light paint.

One important factor in choosing wall color is the color of the floor. The trick is to balance light and dark, not letting one dominate the room. With dark oak flooring, for example, the choice would be light or medium walls. Floors carpeted in a medium tone would offer the option of either light or dark walls; medium or dark walls go well with light-colored floors. As might be expected, a room with a dark floor and light walls and ceiling is apt to appear more open than the same room with medium-toned walls. What if you wanted to lower the apparent ceiling height in a room with a very light floor surface? One approach might be to mount a picture molding around the walls a foot or so below the ceiling break. Then paint the ceiling dark down to the molding and the remainder of the walls a medium color.

Pattern and Space

Like color, pattern has the power to move walls and ceilings in relation to a viewer. Strong vertical patterns can heighten rooms. Small-scale patterns can make a wall seem small and hence farther away; large patterns fill in space. Medium patterns can be a good compromise for a small room with unbroken walls.

It would be oversimplifying, though, to state that big prints close rooms in and little ones open them up. Small, tightly repeating patterns, especially if they are dark, can seem to bring walls closer because of their ability to create texture. Moreover, depending on the manner in which they repeat, even small designs often create distinct vertical or horizontal lines (or, for that matter, diagonal lines, whose effect is to expand space). One crucial factor is background. Regardless of the size of the pattern, a light background expands a room's sense of space, a background with a strong or dark color moves toward the viewer.

Defining a Space

Color and pattern can do more than simply make an area bigger or smaller. Either one can also help you *define* space—that is, deliberately set off an area with paint or wallcovering. In fact, many designers use wallpaper *borders* to carry out this task. Available through most decorator shops, borders are typically sold with fine papers, especially hand-screened designs. In combination with a good paint job, borders can be a surprisingly effective way of accenting a room.

Borders are commonly used to mark a room's perimeter at the ceiling break, but they can be equally effective in other applications. For example, a border can highlight an attractive bedroom closet or the large mirrors in a dining room. Borders can also add real punch to doors and windows, or they can create a headboard where none exists. Just be certain there's enough wall space so the borders don't look crowded. (For more about borders, see page 87.)

There are other ways papers can define space. For example, you can create an attractive dado effect in a dining room by pasting consecutive 30-inch-high strips of wallpaper around its perimeter. Or paste large paper panels at even intervals on your walls, and surround each panel with a well-chosen border or wood molding. Center a picture in each panel and you'll feel as if you've converted your room into an elegant private library.

Paint can also define space. One way is with the power of contrast (see pages 16–17). A complementary or contrasting color helps set off an inset wood panel from its surrounding frame. Another good way to define space is by stenciling a border, a technique described in detail on pages 52–53. Of course, borders can also be painted freehand, if you've got a steady—and artistic—hand.

A charming hand-painted border accents a prominent corner in this monochromatic color scheme (opposite, top). Wallpaper borders would achieve the same effect of defining a space. In the solarium (opposite, bottom), contrasting white trim appears to expand the windows while the dark wall paint, which helps reduce glare, makes the walls recede. The result is a sense of open, airy space.

DESIGN: CONTRAST

Call it interest, spark, liveliness, or what you will, there's a quality that makes some "correctly" designed rooms bland while others exude energy, vitality, and drama. Strip away the words and you'll find in nearly all cases that the patterns and colors in the exciting rooms carry a faint hint of the unexpected—a carefully controlled use of a simple concept: *contrast.*

Scale

Scale—in terms of large and small patterns—can be used to control the feeling of space. It can also create contrast. Obviously, you wouldn't put the same small pattern in every room of the house; it would probably be unwise to repeat it even in a bedroom and adjoining bath. What you can do is combine related papers in

small, medium, and large scales to create excitement without destroying continuity. You'll find a wide variety of wallpaper designs in companion scales.

Pattern

Contrast between patterns themselves can also lead to a more exciting decor. One way to work with contrast in pattern is to view all patterns as either geometrics or florals. Geometrics are characterized by angular lines and florals by curving ones. If you're uncertain which is which, try the squint test: look at the pattern from a few feet away. If the predominant pattern is lines or angles —stripes or diamonds, say—you've got a geometric, *even if the subject matter of the design is actually flowers.* You produce contrast by combining a geometric with a floral. In general, small geometrics combine nicely with medium or large-scale florals; square geometrics juxtaposed with large florals make an especially exciting contrast. You might, therefore, divide the wall in a breakfast nook between a bold stripe pattern on the bottom and a delicate floral on the upper wall, separating the patterns with a chair rail.

Color

Your walls will be more exciting if they feature an inter-

Contrast can be achieved with a crisp, clean white against almost any tone, as in the living room at left, where the woodwork contrasts with a subtle beige. Note the variation in the wall color produced by different sources and quantities of light.

play of light, dark, and medium values. Light-colored monochromatic rooms tend to be spacious but dull; dark-colored monochromatic rooms often suffer from a closed-in feeling and lack of light. The solution is contrast. Contrasting colors command attention from the eyes. That's why our Victorian ancestors, proud of their fine woodwork, often painted the trim a different color from the walls. The principle of color contrast explains why many designers recommend painting the insides of all closets white—any clothing, even dark suits, stands out against such a background.

Materials

Just as changing from dark to light colors automatically creates contrast and thus emphasis, different materials add interest. This is true whether you juxtapose shiny and flat paints, paint and paper, or paper and textured materials, such as fabric. Even if your room is painted all one color, if you use a flat latex paint on the walls and a satin enamel on the trim, the different reflective qualities of the two paints will create some contrast. This is why most designers are sticklers for papering or painting all electrical switch and outlet covers (see page 82) to match the wall. Failure to do so automatically creates contrast, and draws unwanted attention.

As with most design considerations, you can go too far with contrast. Combine more than a single geometric with a floral pattern, for example, and you may end up with confusion rather than contrast. Too much variety in paint and pattern creates choppy, unpleasant spaces. So practice moderation, making a balance of contrast and continuity your goal.

Companion Papers

Contrast produces interest in a room, but too much contrast can be chaotic. Companion papers offer a way to introduce controlled contrast. Many such papers create variety by altering scale or reversing colors. Shown below are two quite different designs that are related by theme—both represent bamboo—and by their identical (and very limited) color scheme.

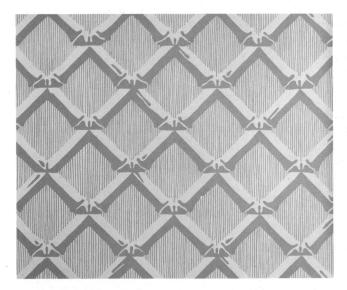

DESIGN: TEXTURE

Texture refers to how coatings and wallcoverings feel —or look like they feel—to the touch. Cork, corduroy, silk, flocked papers, pasted leaves, and even polyethylene have all been used to create textured walls. Texture can be a matter of appearance, as in the case of tight, redundant wallpaper patterns—mini prints, as they are sometimes called—that create a distinct visual texture. Paint can also possess texture. Indeed, some manufacturers mix sand and other materials into their finishes to produce so-called textured paints, which are especially effective in covering damage, or inexpert taping on wallboard walls (see page 30).

Putting a textured covering on your walls can introduce accent and interest in your room. To use texture, apply the same principles of contrast and continuity that govern more conventional coverings. Squint your eyes and even grasscloth may exhibit a small-scale pattern that could benefit from a complementing design. In a family room, for example, a "natural" texture such as burlap on the upper walls might make a good contrast for varnished wood wainscoting. Foil or embossed wallpapers present a strong texture that you shouldn't ignore in planning your decor. In most instances, texture tends to close a space in (this is not true of foil, however, because of its great light-reflective capacity), and, like any accent, texture tends to draw attention to itself. So, as with most aspects of design, strive for proportion and balance.

The hand-painted, paper-backed silk wallcovering gives the walls of the bedroom opposite a warm, tactile feeling. The table beneath the mirror has a painted finish called *faux* stone, much like the false marble technique described on page 50.

A Sampling of Textures

Woven straw

Grasscloth

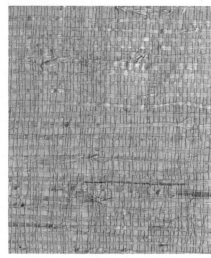

Gold foil

Cork veneer

Mica "pebbles"

Leaves

DESIGN: FABRIC

Fabric on walls has recently become enormously popular. Some designers speculate that fabric and other special wallcoverings help us bring character and detail into homes whose architecture lacks such warming qualities. There are practical advantages to fabric as well. It is often more durable and less expensive than wallpaper. Virtually any type of cloth can be used, from elegant sheets to inexpensive upholstery material such as that employed on the underside of seat cushions. When backed with padding, fabric helps deaden sound, a special attraction to apartment dwellers and those whose neighborhoods tend to be noisy. Fabric may appeal to the renter because it is a less permanent wall treatment than paint or paper. Fabric can also function as a kind of on-the-wall insulation. In the photo on the opposite page, an inexpensive muslin hides damage to the walls of an old home. It was attached with an air-powered stapling gun by means of the technique called backtacking, described on pages 90–91.

The shirred-on-the-rod technique (below, left) makes fabric easy to install and remove for washing or relocation, suiting this wall-treatment approach to apartment dwellers or frequent movers. The gathered curtains in a floral pattern make a pleasing contrast to the ruffled geometric fabric on the walls. (See page 17 for a discussion of geometric and floral patterns.)

Padded fabric wall panels (below, right), which may be cut to any width, are particularly appropriate in large rooms with generous areas of unbroken wall space. The matching fabric panels on the lower part of the wall cover bookcases and help to unify this spacious room.

On the opposite page is an example of backtacking. Gimp, installed with the help of an electric glue gun, hides the staples and creates a strong horizontal line that visually lowers the high ceiling.

DESIGN: THE INTANGIBLES

It may seem that deciding which paint and wallcoverings look best together is largely a matter of following certain prescribed principles governing the use of color and pattern. But if things were that simple, professional designers would long ago have been replaced by computers. In fact, nearly all successful interiors contain additional qualities that can only be described as highly subjective—the intangibles. Style, character, and drama can lift a well-decorated room into the category of the unusual and, on occasion, into the realm of the truly breathtaking.

Style

Style means follow-through, a consistency of design that ties together all the various elements in your room —furniture, lighting, and floor coverings, as well as colors and patterns. Is your room "English," "Country French," "Early American," "Modern"? Whether you've accumulated your furnishings over the years, or you have the good fortune to be able to assemble a coordinated grouping at one time, you'll achieve the most harmonious effect if you choose a specific style and stick to it. You may want to do a bit of research to decide on the colors and patterns most suited to the style of your home.

Character

In terms of color and pattern, character is punch. It's the distinctive touch that makes a room yours, different from another room that has the same paint or wallpaper. It might be evidenced by the choice of wallpaper in a dining room to create a dado, chair rail, paneling, and ceiling cornice; or an off-white paint on the inner surfaces of built-in display shelves. Whatever the specific colors, patterns, or materials involved, character is individual, a personal choice that makes an ordinary room something noteworthy.

Drama

Drama is the world of strong colors and even stronger, more unconventional patterns. Drama is special effects such as false marble and *trompe l'oeil* murals (see pages 50 and 86), bold colors, large patterns, and eye-catching accessories. Light, particularly artificial light, is almost always an ingredient in a room with drama. Sometimes it is achieved by breaking with convention: a small bathroom papered with a large-scale design or painted an intense color, or a long hallway with big horizontal bands of rainbow colors. Drama risks disapproval; it may also achieve stunning beauty and excitement.

Style—a restrained and elegant modern look—is evident in the living room on the opposite page. The limited color scheme of muted grays and pink, the simple window treatment, and the minimum of furniture all contribute to a refined effect. The inherent harmony of this spare, contemporary room comes from the careful selection of each element so that all reflect the consistency that constitutes style.

Drama is the first word that comes to mind at the sight of the red dining room above. From the choice of color—an unadulterated primary spread lavishly over all the walls—with its gleaming finish, to the boldness of more red in the furnishings, it is a design scheme that takes chances. The lacquered effect was created with oil-based enamel topped by a coat of polyurethane varnish.

Character abounds in a Victorian window corner (right), where attention to detail creates a harmonious statement of personal taste. The delicate, tightly patterned design on the walls is paint applied with a roller (see page 50). The windows are painted with the same two tones of brown plus a green touch that is repeated in the curtain ties. The grandfather clock is right at home with the curved lines of this design scheme.

THE FINAL DECISION

The Design Decision

In the previous pages, you've wrestled with the notions of scale and space, continuity and contrast. You've thought about color, pattern, and texture; and you've contemplated complements, climate, and chromatics.

Now, you must put theory to use, seek out your local paint or wallcovering dealer, and make some decisions. First, you should think of the most basic question of all—whether to use paint or wallcovering. Each has advantages. Paint is generally cheaper and easier to work with. In many "problem" situations—very high ceilings or extremely rough textured walls, for example—paint is clearly the finish of choice. Wallcoverings, on the other hand, are usually better at setting a mood, providing texture, camouflaging damage, and drawing attention to a focal point wall. These distinctions may help you choose one over the other. But your final decision may nonetheless be based on feeling as much as logic. That's all right. The more your choice reflects your personality, the more your design will be uniquely yours.

Self-analysis

You have to decide what you can live with. Some people enjoy stronger color and patterns than others do. Look around your own home. What kind of artwork and furniture do you have? If you tend toward off-white and neutral gray, you're not likely to want to make a strong statement. If, on the other hand, you line your walls with Cezanne and Matisse posters, chances are you'll be comfortable with more color.

Some things, of course, are givens. Important elements of structural design or the outdoor environment influence your interior decor. But what about other design decisions that may have been made for you? You may be stuck with a houseful of carpeting you don't like, but can't afford to replace. If you want to display artwork, you'll limit yourself to colors and patterns that don't detract from the paintings. Similarly, if your home boasts truly compelling architecture, you may want to avoid wallpaper, passing up complicated patterns in favor of simple colors that accentuate and enhance the structure's lines. Or your furniture may dictate a certain kind of wallcovering.

Beyond whatever constraints you may have to cope with, you must be precise in thinking about what it is you wish to do. That means being more specific than simply wanting to cover old paint and wallpaper. Are you trying to add character to an area? Create a mood or style? Provide a backdrop for artwork or other collectibles? Cover damaged walls? Give yourself a little time to think this through—you may surprise yourself by discovering that, in fact, you're ready for a dramatic room. So do it, based on your personal style. And be realistic, considering things you can't change, such as the size of your pocketbook.

Being Practical

Of course, not every dream can come true. It's necessary to consider the practical aspects of your choice as well.

How much can you afford to spend? Do you have enough money to paint or wallpaper the entire room? Clearly, economics is more of an issue with wallcoverings than with paint. Hand-screened wallpapers can sell for $50 or more per roll. That would come to almost $750 for material alone in a room requiring 14 rolls of paper, about what you might need for an average size bedroom. Fabric coverings can be as much or more—professionals figure covering a room in standard, 54-inch-wide designer fabric generally costs about twice as much as it would to do the same job in hand-screened paper. Even if you decide to paint, you may have budget problems. Some accent paints sell for as much as $40 per gallon.

Budgeting is crucial because if you don't think through how much you have to spend, you may come to the end of your money before you complete your job. Plan how many wall surfaces you can afford to paint or paper. What about the ceilings? Use the formulas on pages 33, 63, and 89 to calculate accurately how much of a given material you'll need. With paper, don't forget the cost-saving option of borders (see page 87). Or, if your financial situation is really tight, what about covering just one or two walls?

When planning your expenditures, remember that with most wallcovering and paint materials, you'll get more or less what you pay for. So always shop carefully and purchase the best quality materials your budget can afford. Sacrificing quality—in paint, wallpaper, or fabric—is a false economy that may well come back to haunt you in a job that doesn't stand up to time.

There are other factors, both practical and subjective, to consider in addition to budget. For instance, you'll need to strike a realistic compromise between practical and esthetic considerations. Suede might be the best-looking wallcovering possible for a given bedroom, but if the bedroom belongs to a child, you'd better start thinking in terms of more durable alternatives. Similarly, vinyl paper is probably a better choice than flat latex paint in heavy-traffic areas like hallways and corridors. Stencil painting your floors can be a wonderful design touch, but consider, for all the effort you put into it—will it last long enough?

Working With Your Dealer

Find a well-stocked wallpaper and/or paint store with knowledgeable clerks and salespeople, and become a loyal and familiar customer, even if it means paying a bit more. You'll be rewarded by fewer mistakes and a longer-lasting, higher-quality job. The clearer you are about what you want, the more your dealer will be able to help you. Always take samples along, even if it's just a small patch of carpet or a paint chip. With those simple items in hand, and having carefully thought through the job you're trying to accomplish, the final decision will emerge naturally, and you'll be on your way to the satisfaction of a new look that's exactly right.

The following questions will help you bring into focus the issues you need to resolve before you start purchasing paint or wallcoverings.

1. Have you decided how many rooms you will eventually paint or paper? First think about the entire house, then tackle it room by room. Put enough time into planning ahead so that you don't start a job until you know exactly what you're going to do. And be realistic in defining the scope of your project—don't try redoing the living room, dining room, and den over a single weekend.

2. What do you want the wallcovering or paint to do for the rooms you have selected? The preceding pages give you some idea of what they can do: add character; create mood or style; provide an easily maintained surface; "bridge" colors; define a space; add texture; add drama; create a backdrop for art or collectibles; cover damaged walls; add light; and add dimension.

The more purposes you can identify, the more specific you can be about the wall treatment you want. For example, if you'd like to cover up damaged walls, add light, *and* add texture, you might settle very quickly on a shiny, shirred-on-the-rod fabric (see pages 92–93).

3. How will one room relate to the next? Keep in mind the principle of balancing continuity and contrast. You can mix and match a number of variables to interrelate your rooms: paper and paint, scale, texture, lighting, warm and cool colors, light and dark colors, floral and geometrical patterns, shiny and flat finishes.

4. What colors are already in your home? What colors would you like to add? What colors do you want to play down? Take samples with you when you shop. If you have a problem obtaining a sample of your existing paint or wallcovering, get a set of manufacturer's chips (available from most dealers), find one that matches, and carry it along.

5. What about practical considerations? Now's the time to stop any wishful thinking and settle on the finish that makes the most sense. You may decide to stress durability. Or budget constraints may mean that some rooms receive only a fresh coat of the existing paint rather than the coordinated fabric and wallpaper you'd like. Plan out quite carefully what your expenses will be, where and how you'll economize, what you'll do first, and what you'll postpone.

Paint and Wallcovering Shoppers' Guide

Armed with answers to the questions above, you're ready to prepare a personal chart like the one shown below. Even if you hire a professional painter or paperhanger, it's a good idea to prepare such a guide first. Although it may seem like a lot of trouble, the effort will be rewarded in a paint or wallcovering treatment suited to your unique needs and personality. (Information on figuring how much paint you'll need can be found on page 33; for paper, see page 63; for fabric, see page 89.)

Rooms to paint or paper	Objective(s)	Existing colors that will remain (attach samples)	Proposed replacements or additions (attach samples)	How much needed?
Living room	Add drama; coordinate with dining room	Oatmeal carpeting	Light and dark blue paper, nonvinyl, formal floral, large scale.	20 rolls
			White trim.	1 gallon
Dining room	Make backdrop for art; coordinate with living room	Oatmeal carpeting; formal dark wood table, chairs, and buffet	Soft beige latex paint. Small-scale geometric paper in beige and white.	2 gallons 14 rolls
			White trim.	1 gallon
Bedroom	Add feeling of space; coordinate with existing drapes and bedspread	Oatmeal carpeting; multicolored drapes; dark blue bedspread	White latex paint for ceiling.	1 gallon
			Pale blue (color from drapes) latex paint for walls.	2 gallons

PAINTING

Step-by-step illustrations and instructions
show you how to select good-quality paint,
prepare surfaces, and get the best results from
brushes, pads, rollers, and sprayers.
A special section gives directions on
using glazes and stencils.

Paint is probably the cheapest and easiest way to alter the appearance of your home. With a free weekend and a can of paint, you can add drama, style, and personality to a room faster than with almost any other kind of redecorating. At the least, you can freshen a faded color scheme; you may even change the colors completely. With a well-prepared surface, paint can also help hide structural flaws, alter spatial characteristics, or add the look of Old World detail to otherwise plain surroundings.

Paint isn't new. The use of coatings for decorative and protective purposes can be traced to the Ice Age, when red, yellow, and charcoal earth colors were used in cave drawings. The early Egyptians produced pigments from natural ores such as lime, alumina, and soda ash; and natural substances used by the Greeks and Romans produced paints of such durability that some examples survive to this day. American Indians made white paint by chewing salmon eggs and tree bark and then blending in the ashes of deer bones and antlers.

All paint is a mixture of pigment, binder, and thinner. Together, the binders and thinner are known as the paint's *vehicle*; when the thinner evaporates, the paint is dry. The proportion of the three basic components can be changed to produce paints with varying characteristics; for example, reducing the amount of solvent has lengthened drying times and, many professional painters insist, decreased the durability of petroleum-based paints.

Buying Paint

Today an often bewildering array of paints confronts the do-it-yourselfer. There are interior and exterior coatings, alkyds, latexes, glazes, epoxy paints, dripless gels,

acoustical paints, sprays, sealers, and shiny and flat paints (see page 28 for definitions of painting terms). In most instances, however, you need only consider two kinds of finishes: oil-based paints (also called alkyds) and water-based paints (also called latexes). Each has distinct advantages and disadvantages that you'll want to consider carefully. For a review of types of paints, see pages 30–31.

Preparation

Whichever finish coating you choose, what happens beneath the surface will be even more important. Success will depend on the care and effort you put into preparation. That means sanding, patching, priming, and all the other unglamorous tasks that must be carried out before you even think about brushing on finish paint. Proper preparation can determine whether the paint you apply to woodwork sticks or flakes off after a few weeks or months; whether patched cracks or holes in your walls blend in or draw unwanted attention. Most professional painters budget at least one third of their time to preparation. So should you. For preparation specifics, see pages 36–41.

Primers. While latex paints can be applied over oil-based paints and vice versa, for a good job using either paint, you should start with a primer. You could use two coats of finish paint, but primers do a better job of sealing off underlying surfaces and providing "tooth"—a rough surface to which the finish paint can adhere. Moreover, primers are usually cheaper than premium finish paints. Latex primer should be used for unpainted wallboard; for any other surface, most professionals prefer an oil-based undercoat for both latex and alkyd finishes. See pages 30 and 33 for more information on primers.

Tools, Materials, and Techniques

Besides well-prepared surfaces, of course, successful painting requires proper materials, techniques, and tools. In the pages that follow, you'll find information on each of these. You'll even get an introduction to some dazzling special effects you can create with your own paint brush (pages 50–53).

In a small living room, a monochromatic scheme of soft pink is a space-expanding device. Combined with matching fabric and a coordinated floor treatment, it is also a romantic mood-setter. The walls were deliberately not smoothed, for contrast with the elegant texture of the sofas.

THE LANGUAGE OF PAINT

Acrylic
A plasticlike resin used to bind pigment, water, and other ingredients in latex paint.

Alkali
A substance commonly found in masonry surfaces, which tends to leach through paint coatings.

Alkyd
An oil-based paint made with synthetic resins. All interior oil-based paints today are alkyds.

Binder
The ingredient that holds together the components of paint; modern paints, whether water-based or oil-based, use resins for binding. In general, the more resin in a paint, the greater its durability.

Calcimine
A water-based paint formerly used for ceilings. Any calcimine coat *must* be covered with primer before another paint can be applied.

Caulking
A flexible filler for open joints. Caulking materials, as distinct from patching compounds, are primarily employed to seal out air or water rather than to prepare a surface for painting.

Ceiling paint
A thick, flat coating, sometimes tinted to reduce glare, made especially for painting ceilings.

Cutting in
Painting the edges of a wall or ceiling area. See page 43.

Deglossing
Any means of abrading a surface about to be painted. See page 39 for a discussion of liquid deglossers.

Enamel
Paint that dries with a glossy or semiglossy finish.

Epoxy
A plasticlike paint that dries by means of chemical action (rather than evaporation) to an extremely hard surface. See page 30.

Feathering
Thinning the outer edges of a patched or painted area by sanding or by stroking with a relatively dry brush, respectively.

Glaze
A thin mixture of oil and mineral spirits, usually tinted when applied, used to achieve special painting effects. See page 50.

Gloss
Shininess—that is, capacity for reflecting light. Glossy paints contain more binder resins than flat finishes have. Flat paints resist glare, which is especially useful on uneven surfaces. Semigloss paints are shinier and more stain- and wash-resistant and are useful on trim or in kitchens and bathrooms. Glossy paints are highest in luster and are useful for furniture and extremely high-wear trim areas.

Latex
A paint whose resins, pigment, and other ingredients are suspended in water.

Masking
Shielding an area from paint, usually with tape or paint guides.

Mildew
A splotchy fungus that flourishes in high-moisture areas and can stain or mar finishes. See page 38.

Mineral spirits
Petroleum-based paint thinner.

Muriatic acid
A diluted form of hydrochloric acid used to clean alkali deposits from masonry. Muriatic acid is a dangerous substance and should be used only under safe conditions. See page 48.

Patching compound
A plasterlike material used to fill cracks and holes in plaster, wallboard, and wood.

Polyurethane
An extremely durable clear plastic finish, used for floors, trim, and other woodwork.

Pouncing
A technique for dispersing paint throughout the bristles of a brush by repeatedly flexing it against a surface such as newspaper. Pouncing is used for special effects such as marbling techniques.

Primer
A gritty undercoat designed to help finish paint adhere and cover. There are latex and oil-based primers, shellac-based primer-sealers, and primers for metal surfaces.

Putty knife
A spatula used for applying patching compounds and scraping wood. Broader-bladed versions are known as "taping" or simply "broad" knives, and are used for applying joint compound to wallboard as well as for larger patch repairs.

Resins
The prime binding agent of most modern paints. Resin was initially derived from the natural secretions of certain plants and insects (see "Shellac") but today is synthetically produced in forms such as alkyds, acrylics, and urethanes.

Shellac
A clear, glossy finish made by dissolving in alcohol the resinous secretions of scale insects. Shellac is extremely easy to apply and repair, but cannot be used over other finishes and is easily marred by alcohol or water.

Solvent
A liquid in which a paint or other coating can be dissolved; used to improve flow of paint when brushing and to clean paint from applicators and other gear.

Stippling
A technique for blending fresh paint with an older coat or for matching the texture of a patch to that of the surrounding wall. To do stippling, the brush is held perpendicular to the surface being painted and the ends of the bristles are tapped quickly and lightly against the surface.

Trisodium phosphate (TSP)
A strong, water-soluble cleaning agent that is useful in degreasing walls and in other heavy cleanup. Can also be used as a deglossing agent on wood before priming and painting.

Turpentine
A thinner, like mineral spirits, but derived from pine trees.

Varnish
A transparent finish, chiefly used on natural wood surfaces.

PAINTING SAFELY

When preparing surfaces and applying paint finishes you often use chemicals and procedures that present serious safety hazards. Year after year, for example, falls from ladders are a leading cause of household injuries. Here are some basic guidelines that will reduce the chances of a mishap.

Do secure all scaffolds. When you set a plank on ladders or sawhorses, be sure it extends a foot beyond them, and clamp or nail the plank to its supports.

Do rub protective skin lotion into your hands, arms, and neck before painting, and clean up thoroughly as soon as possible after painting.

Do wear rubber gloves when handling strong agents such as liquid deglosser or trisodium phosphate (TSP).

Do protect your eyes *at all times*. Wear glasses or safety goggles when doing *any* overhead work such as painting or patching of ceilings. Wear glasses or goggles when clearing plaster dust from walls and wallboard. Never rub your fingers in your eyes after handling strong solvents.

Do keep all pets out of a painting area.

Do use solvents in well-ventilated areas only.

Do turn off all sources of flame, including pilot lights, when spraying any solvent-containing paint.

Do keep all paint products out of the reach of children.

Do keep your work area free of debris that could cause tripping or falling.

Do set aside a proper place for storing tools and materials not in use.

Don't climb any stepladder unless its spreader bars are locked in place and both pairs of legs are fully open.

Don't climb higher on any ladder than the second step from the top. If that isn't close enough to your work, you need a taller ladder.

Don't use too steep an angle when bracing a ladder against a wall. The ladder could pull away from the wall when you climb it. The safe recommendation is: the distance between the feet of the ladder and the wall should be one fourth the height of the ladder.

Don't use aluminum ladders near electrical wires.

Don't use solvent near a flame or fire. Don't smoke when using solvents.

Don't ignore the safety precautions printed on paint cans. Read and follow them carefully.

Don't operate a paint sprayer in *any* manner other than as instructed. See page 49 for more information on sprayer safety.

Don't store oil- or solvent-soaked rags. Rinse and dispose of them carefully. If you must store used rags, thoroughly wash them beforehand. See page 55 for more information on paint storage.

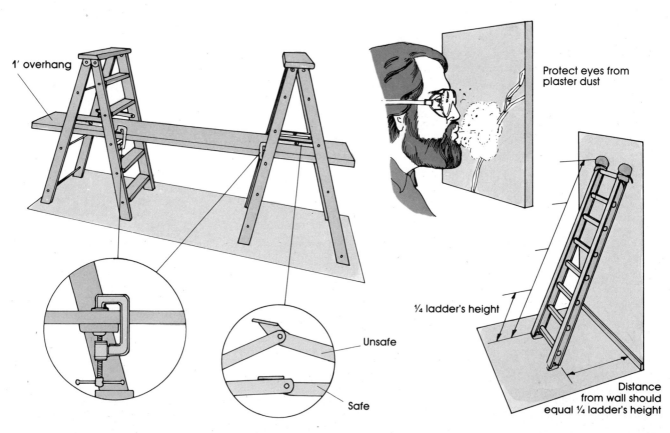

1' overhang

Protect eyes from plaster dust

¼ ladder's height

Unsafe

Safe

Distance from wall should equal ¼ ladder's height

TYPES OF PAINT

Oil-based and Water-based Paints
To begin with at least, let's define the world of paint as neatly bipolar, consisting solely of water-based, or latex, and oil-based, or alkyd, finishes. Other paints are discussed below, but for most jobs, you'll be choosing between oil-based and water-based finishes. Each has distinct advantages and drawbacks.

Oil-based Finishes

Until the mid-1950s, nearly all finishes, including flat wall paints, had oil bases. (Oil-based paints are often called alkyds because of their binder, a synthetic resin.) Alkyds stick to smooth surfaces better than latexes and are more washable and longer lasting than their water-based counterparts. Thus, oil-based paints are still the coatings of choice for woodwork, especially in high-wear areas, and for special situations, such as painting in cold temperatures or over smoke- or water-stained walls.

Unfortunately, oil-based paints also possess significant disadvantages. Cleanup requires messy, flammable thinners. Many of today's alkyds contain less solvent, so they aren't as durable as their forerunners and take longer to dry. Oil-based paints give off strong fumes; any room painted with an oil finish must be well ventilated until the paint is dry.

Water-based Finishes

Water-based finishes, or latexes, generally have little odor, and cleanup requires only soap and water. Latex paints dry to the touch much faster than oil-based paints. Latex paints now account for nearly all flat wall paint sold. They are available in both interior and exterior enamel finishes as well. Exterior latex enamels can sometimes be substituted to advantage indoors, according to some professionals; however, whether they leave fewer brush marks and stand up better to scrubbing is open to debate. Their color range is limited.

Primers

The complexity of primers reflects the wide diversity of finish materials. Special rust-inhibiting zinc- and oil-based primers exist for painting steel, aluminum, and other household metal items. Masonry primers form a protective barrier against water seepage or fill holes in porous concrete (see page 48). Many of today's best primers are marketed as "stain killers" or "stain locking" finishes, because they are effective in sealing out water or smoke damage. Aerosol primers are handy for making small patches in walls and woodwork. For most jobs you will be choosing between water-based and oil-based primers. Always check with your dealer to make certain the primer you choose is compatible with your finish coat.

Special Paints
Sometimes—when you're trying to paint ceramic tile or a metal cabinet, for example—ordinary oil- or water-based paints simply can't do the job. Fortunately, a number of special finishes are available, but they are expensive. See page 48 for a description of special coatings for masonry and page 94 for a discussion of natural wood finishes.

Epoxy Paint

Epoxy paints are especially effective on nonporous surfaces such as porcelain, ceramic tile, plastic, and metal. The strongest epoxy paints are mixed in two parts and offer extremely high adhesion and scratch- and scrub-resistance. Epoxy paints require a well-prepared surface and special solvents for cleanup. Because of their fast-drying properties, epoxies can leave brush marks.

Ceiling Paint

Most people paint their ceilings with the same flat latex coatings they use on their walls. But for ceilings that have been deeply stained or repeatedly patched, the greater hiding power of special ceiling paints may be worth their higher cost. Because of their thickness, ceiling paints tend to drip less and can cover in a single coat. They should not be confused with *acoustical* ceiling paint, a special finish that is usually sprayed on and is designed to improve the sound-deadening ability of painted acoustical tile.

Textured Paints

The thick consistency of textured flat oil or latex paints can be especially effective in camouflaging walls flawed by damage or too-visible taping of wallboard. Textured paint can be applied to the surface with a carpet roller or "skip-troweled" (skimmed on with a plasterer's trowel) to create a rough finish. Another textured finish, sand paint—a latex paint containing sand or a sand substitute—looks like grainy concrete when dry and can help reduce ceiling glare. Because of their porosity, surfaces covered with textured and sand paints tend to soak up more paint if later recoated with a regular finish.

Heat-resistant Paint

Oil-based heat-resistant paints are specially designed for metal objects subject to high temperatures and can turn everyday objects, such as fireplace screens and hoods, radiators, steam pipes, and gas heater grills, into attractive room accents. Available in a limited selection of flat colors, heat-resistant paints usually act as their own primers. Underlying surfaces must be clean and free of rust.

Metal Primers and Finish Paints

These special paints are for metal surfaces, where prevention of corrosion and adequate adhesion must both be provided. Such primers used to contain red or blue lead, but now use zinc chromate, which is yellow.

CHOOSING THE RIGHT PAINT

Choosing Colors

Even if you know exactly what *kind* of paint you want, how can you be certain about color? Having picked the color we think we want (see pages 6–7), few of us can memorize that color and recall it with precision when we get to the store. Even if we could, many colors—greens and rusts, for example—vary perceptibly depending on their surroundings. Colors can be influenced by the degree to which the interior reflects outside colors —greenery near a window, perhaps, or a large back-yard pool—and by lighting conditions—direct or in-direct sunlight, incandescent or fluorescent light—some of which change with the time of day.

In addition, the *kind* of paint and the surface on which it is painted may significantly affect the appearance of paint. The same color often looks deeper in glossy paints than in flat paints, for example, On the other hand, an especially porous surface can flatten a paint intended to have a sheen.

Given the changeability of color, how are you to buy the paint you want? When you made your design plan, you probably chose a very particular color. When you go to the paint dealer, take with you anything that helps identify that color: a bit of wallpaper or a snippet from the seam of a drape, for instance, or your daughter's favorite dress, if that's what gave you the inspiration. This will be a first step toward finding the color you want.

Evaluating color. The small sample colors or "chips" provided by most manufacturers are essential in shaping your initial design decisions, but they aren't enough to make a final color selection. For that, you'll need to invest in a small can of paint for each color you plan to use in the room, including wall paint and trim. Pick a highly visible spot (you'll prime out the area later) that receives light typical for the room as a whole. Apply the paint to the same surface on which it will be used as a finish coat. For wall paint, daub on a sample about three to four brush widths across and 3 feet long. For trim, brush a 3-foot run of paint along the door frame or over some mid-wall paneling.

Now, let the sample coatings dry *thoroughly*. Wait several days before you buy any more paint—long enough for a complete evaluation. Note how the color ties in with your existing furnishings. Does the color clash or harmonize with your sofa or bedspread? Observe the paint swatches at different times of the day. If they change color, does that affect the relationship between the paint and the other major decor elements such as carpets and drapes?

Correcting the color. What if you don't like the color you've chosen? Even if it's only off by a bit, ask your dealer to change the paint's tint (with today's paint costs as high as they are, it's probably best to leave any actual mixing of paint colors and pigments to your dealer). If the color seems completely inappropriate, however, you may have to choose a new paint and a fresh spot on the wall and start all over again.

Priming for color. Most professionals recommend that you always prime (see page 33). But it can be especially important if the color you've chosen differs sharply from the preexisting one. Without a primer coat the underlying color may show through the new coat of paint.

What Kind of Paint Should You Choose?

	Plaster ceilings and walls	Wallboard ceilings and walls	Wood trim, cabinets, shelves	Metal trim
Living room, dining room, bedroom	Oil-based primer Flat latex finish coat	Latex primer, if new and unpainted Oil-based primer, if already finished Flat latex finish coat	Varnish or Oil-based primer Oil-based finish coat	Metal primer Oil-based or latex finish coat
Kitchen, bathroom	Oil-based primer Oil-based finish coat	Latex primer, if new and unpainted Oil-based primer, if already finished Oil-based finish coat	Varnish or Oil-based primer Oil-based finish coat	Metal primer Oil-based finish coat
	Concrete floors and walls			
Basement, garage	Sealer or special masonry primer Latex masonry paint		Varnish or Oil-based primer Oil-based finish coat	Metal primer Oil-based finish coat

BUYING PAINT

Although the world of paint can basically be divided into water-based and oil-based finishes, the qualities and mixtures of paint are separate, more complex issues. The cost and quality of paint have been deeply affected by spiraling oil prices, general inflation, and government regulation, so shopping wisely for paint is a tougher job than it used to be. You'll need to look closely at the kinds, quality, and ingredients of paint. You may even need to stick your finger—or your nose—into the can. And the prepainting tasks of surface preparation are more important than ever.

Paint Lines or Grades

To begin with, most paint companies offer at least three "lines" or grades of paint. By whatever name, the top line consists of *premium paints*, containing the most expensive pigments and binders. Though slightly lower in quality, a middle line—sometimes designated a *decorator* grade—contains a range of pigments and bases similar to the premium line. Nearly all companies also sell a *professional* line, which, despite its name, is usually the lowest in price and quality. Marketed primarily to contractors, professional paints generally rely on clays and other inexpensive inert compounds for covering power.

Paint Mixtures

Within their separate lines of paints, most companies also offer different paint mixtures.

Custom color mixtures. These paints, which have the widest choice of colors for interior painting, are usually available in premium and decorator grades. Literally hundreds of different shades may be chosen from the chips in a single dealer's color selection system. To maintain such a huge inventory in individual cans, your neighborhood paint store would have to be the size of a city block. Instead, the dealer stocks a range of tinting bases, basically a white paint. When a customer requests a given color, the dealer mixes in the necessary pigment, called liquid color, following a predetermined formula. Deep and ultradeep paints get more pigment; pastels and off-whites get less.

Standard factory finishes. These are premixed paints, usually available in all three grades. Factory finishes have a limited color selection, but boast an important advantage. Their pigments, in the form of a dry powder, are mixed in at the factory, and are thus more thoroughly integrated into the paint. As a result, coat for coat, factory finishes resist fading better than their tinted-in-the-store custom counterparts. This can be an important consideration if you're painting a room—a solarium perhaps—that is exposed to strong sunlight for much of the day.

Accent paints. These are factory-prepared pure solid colors—red, yellow, blue, black, and so on—meant to be intermixed to achieve richer tones and greater durability. They are usually sold strictly as premium coatings. For the most part, accent intermixes are used outside, where weathering and fading take their greatest toll. But accent paints can be effective inside as well, if you're striving for a deep color effect or painting a dark color in an unusually sunny room. For example, suppose your color scheme calls for an especially rich burgundy. Your dealer could use red, black, and blue accents—intermixed according to the company's formula—to achieve a depth of color not possible with white-based custom paints or a standard factory finish.

Ask your dealer about using custom, standard, or accent finishes in your particular application. In general, custom colors offer the widest range of choice for most applications, but standard factory coatings cost the least. The price of intermixed accent paints can be double that of even a premium custom color.

Quality of Paint

As leading consumer publications have noted, paint quality has declined recently, at least partly because of the rising prices of raw materials. Some manufacturers have reformulated their paints to include less pigment and titanium dioxide; others are substituting clays for costly acrylics. Nearly all paint makers are cutting back on petroleum-derived solvents. In some instances, however, you can compensate for these changes, with the help of a cooperative and knowledgeable dealer.

For example, some companies reduced the amount of titanium dioxide, a white powder that provides hiding power for many light-range paints, especially whites, off-whites, and pastels. In some cases, you may be able to put it back in to improve coverability. Talk to your dealer about adding a few ounces of titanium the next time you purchase a gallon of light-colored paint; don't try to do it yourself. (Be sure the dealer adjusts the paint formula to allow for the slight change in color.)

Similarly, companies have substituted increasing amounts of clay for acrylic resins in less-than-top-of-the-line latex products, including so-called professional paints. Probably your only defense is to spend more. You'll find the extra cost a good investment. Clay-heavy paints tend to be grainier and less flexible when dry and hence more difficult to wash and touch up after the job is over.

Testing Paint Quality

Actual percentages of binders and hiding pigment are not listed on many paint cans, but you can try some easy tests to determine the quality of paint.

The stick test. Drop a stick into a well-stirred paint can and lift it straight out. Does the paint cling to the stick or run right off? Ideally, 1/8 inch to 1/4 inch of paint should remain on the stick when it is allowed to run off freely. If the paint immediately runs back into the can, it is probably too thin. If, on the other hand, the paint simply sits on the stick without flowing off, it is probably too thick, meaning you may have to purchase and apply more paint than necessary.

The finger test. Rub a little paint between your fingers. It should cling to your skin with enough tenacity to leave a film between your fingers. If the paint simply slides off without leaving any film, it's too thin.

The smell test. The smell of an oil-based paint won't

really tell you much about the paint, though if you have a sensitive nose the smell may influence how easily *you* can work with the paint. On the other hand, the smell of a latex paint can be crucial. Sour-smelling latex paints shouldn't be used (especially if the paint has inadvertently been frozen), as the ingredients are subject to rot. You won't have to sniff for long; if it has turned, latex paint smells like curdled milk.

Choosing a Primer

If you want a good smooth job, start with a primer. It is possible to use two coats of finish paint, but primer is preferable because it does a better job of sealing off underlying surfaces; it provides a uniform surface that supports your finish paint; in most cases it dries faster than ordinary paint; and it's usually cheaper. Use latex primer for unpainted wallboard (a polyvinyl sealer known as PVA is usually recommended); for other surfaces, use an oil-based undercoat for both latex and alkyd finishes. Some professionals believe that untinted oil-based primers are preferable to the tinted variety. Aerosol primers are useful for small areas such as patches and woodwork but are not recommended for full-scale jobs.

Be sure to check with your dealer that the primer you choose is compatible with your finish paint.

Price and Sales

The prices of all paint products have risen rapidly over the past few years, and, as with most products, you get what you pay for. However, paint quality varies considerably from company to company and even within lines and individual finishes. Talk to friendly painting contractors about their favorites when it comes to quality. Read consumer publications that rate the performance of various national paint companies (but don't overlook the possibility that coatings produced by some local manufacturers may be just as good or better).

Always buy the best possible paint you can afford; its price will be small compared to the time you invest in a good job. Figure on spending around $20 per gallon for premium oil-based paint, a few dollars less for a top-grade latex. Add $1 for gloss or semigloss. Don't be fooled by heavy sales promotions or ridiculously low-priced paints; they were probably only medium- to low-quality finishes to begin with. In short, learn all you can about the paint you buy. You may be living with it for a long time.

How Much Paint Do I Need?

1. Measure the length and width of your room and compute the perimeter. If your room is 12 feet wide and 15 feet long, for example, its perimeter is 12 + 12 + 15 + 15 = 54 feet.

2. Multiply the room's perimeter by its height to yield the total wall area in square feet.

3. Subtract 21 square feet for each door and 15 square feet for each normal-sized single window.

4. Divide by 300 (the square feet normally covered by a typical gallon of paint) to get the number of gallons you'll need.

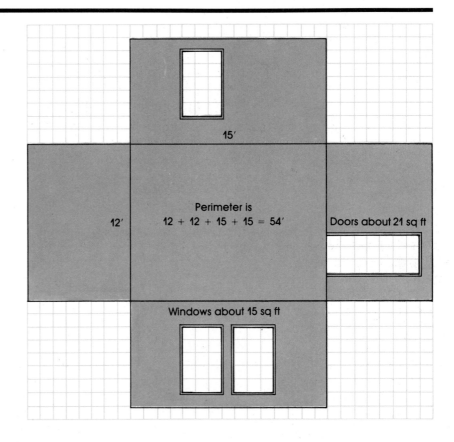

15'

12'

Perimeter is
12 + 12 + 15 + 15 = 54'

Doors about 21 sq ft

Windows about 15 sq ft

Always purchase a little more paint than you need. If, for instance, you're buying 2 quarts—and certainly if you're buying 3—you should probably get a full gallon. For one thing, color can vary from one batch to another. Moreover, some surfaces soak up more paint than you planned for; plaster walls can be far more absorbent than wallboard, for example. If you know you've got a highly porous surface, lower your dividing figure for Step 4 to 250. You should probably buy extra paint if your room has built-in bookshelves and cabinets, because you may wish to paint their interiors. And it's good to have extra paint for future touching up.

TOOLS & MATERIALS

These are some of the tools you'll need for a good-sized painting job. You may find you also want some items that aren't shown—for example, an extension handle for roller-painting a ceiling (see opposite) or a stepladder. Whatever tools you buy, get good ones and keep them clean.

Angled sash brush. For precise painting of narrow surfaces, window frames, moldings, etc.

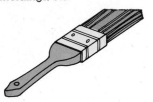

Crack opener. For widening and undercutting plaster cracks.

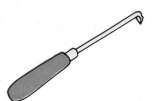

1½-inch putty knife. For general scraping, flaking, and wood filling.

6-inch broad knife. For filling in and smoothing patching compounds in wallboard and plaster repairs.

9-inch roller. For walls and ceilings.

4-inch brush. For "cutting in" walls and large, flat wood surfaces.

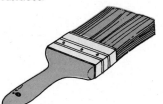

3-inch brush (natural bristle). For wood door moldings, baseboards, etc. Only for oil-based paints.

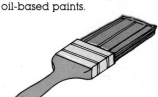

1½-inch brush. For general wood trim.

Masking tape. For protecting windows from paint.

Paint scrapers (hook and straight blade). For removing loose paint from wood and plaster.

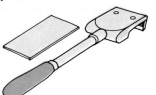

Wire brush. For smoothing fine paint blisters and cracks and roughing up a surface before painting.

Pole sander. For easier sanding of ceilings or large areas.

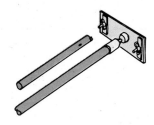

Painting guide. For masking baseboard and other trim areas.

Wire brush comb. For cleaning paint brushes.

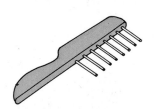

Tack cloth. For wiping dust from woodwork, especially useful with natural wood finishes.

Drop cloths. For covering furniture and floors.

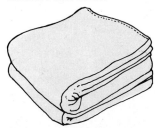

Sponge. For general cleanup of latex paint.

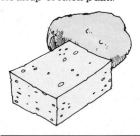

2-gallon pail. For mixing paint.

Painter's mitt. For painting hand rails, pipes, etc.

Roller tray and grid. For loading paint on roller.

Choosing a Brush

Paint brushes can be purchased with either synthetic or natural boar hair "China" bristles. The latter are suitable for use only with oil-based paints (their fibers are hollow and will swell in water). Whichever type, good-quality brushes exhibit the same basic qualities:

☐ flagging: the bristles have split ends, yielding a finer brush stroke.

☐ chiseling: the bristles are graduated in length so that the tip of the brush tapers in and makes an even line when lightly pressed on a flat surface.

☐ flex: the bristles bend more at their tips than at their base, easily shape to contours, and quickly spring back. Flex is related to length. Ordinarily, a brush's bristles should be half again as long as its width.

Before you buy any brush, spread out the bristles and see how they are seated into the heel. Any brush will lose a few bristles, but a poorly constructed brush will shed its bristles right into your paint job. Gaps in the bristles are a sign of poor construction. A good brush is a permanent tool. With proper care it can be used over again many times.

Choosing a Roller

Scrimping on rollers is also a penny-wise, pound-foolish philosophy. A cheap roller can smear your paint by turning too slowly or spatter it by spinning too fast; a poor-quality roller cover will spread paint in uneven splotches. Look for a handle with a 9-inch-wide metal cage frame that turns on nylon bearings and has a comfortable plastic grip threaded for an extension pole. (Avoid handles that require you to remove screws in order to replace a cover; you'll find doing so a nuisance.) Choose a good synthetic cover—they cost about half as much as lambswool—with a plastic core. Use a short-nap cover (¼ inch deep from core to surface) when applying glossy finishes on smooth surfaces, ¾-inch nap for most other work.

A plastic or metal grid, also called a screen, can help ensure that your roller is evenly loaded. The grids can be used in trays or inside 5-gallon pails or cans (the setup most pros prefer for painting areas larger than one room); just be sure the screen is the same width as your roller. Keep it clean—a clogged grid can't draw paint off effectively.

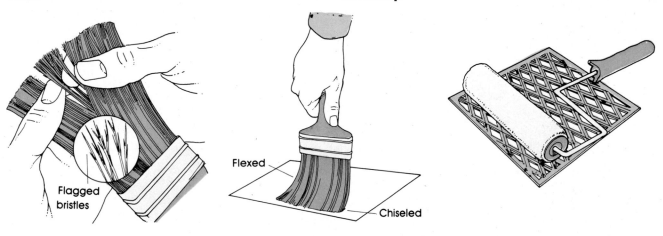

Flagged bristles

Flexed

Chiseled

Special Tools

Specially designed rollers and brushes can help you handle difficult situations. Some rollers, for example, come with very long handles and narrower-than-normal covers—just right for getting behind toilet tanks and into other hard-to-reach places. If you're tall, an *extended frame*—an ordinary roller with longer shank—can eliminate your need for a ladder, even when painting an 8-foot ceiling. If you're on the short side, or your ceilings are higher, get an *extension handle*. The old-fashioned single-piece wood types are steadier than handles that telescope, but the latter can be useful if you are working at varying extension lengths. For a handy tool you can make yourself, saw the handle off a 2- or 3-inch brush to ease the chore of painting inside wood cabinets. There are, of course, a plethora of other *gadgets*, ranging from power-feed rollers to a roller that doubles as a brush (the bristles are built into the core). None of these tools, however, eliminates the need for hard work and careful attention to technique.

Shortened handle

Professional painters learn early to step back and survey their work before starting. You should do the same; stand in the center of the room and identify damaged areas that will need preparation before you paint.

For example, priming both before and after patching will ensure that repairs stay in place and don't absorb paint, which can create an uneven finish. Use the proper sandpaper; 60- to 80-grit silicon carbide is a good choice for plaster or wallboard work. When you use fast-drying patch material, wash all tools immediately to avoid the difficult job of cleaning off hardened compound. Wait until patches are fully dry before applying subsequent layers. Always wear glasses or safety goggles when clearing away plaster or wallboard dust. It's also advisable to wear a dust mask or respirator when doing extensive sanding.

Fixing Plaster Cracks

1. Undercut the crack so that it is wider at its base than at its surface. Undercutting helps keep the patching material in place. You can use a special widening tool available from paint stores or an ordinary can opener. Vacuum or brush out the crack so that it is dust free; tiny particulates are an enemy of strong adhesion.

2. Dampen the plaster in and around the crack. Moving your putty knife downward, press patching compound firmly into and under the edges of the opening. Since you'll often need two layers of compound—the first layer may shrink due to heat, for example—you should leave a rough surface on the first layer. Feather the final layer into the surrounding plaster, sand, and prime.

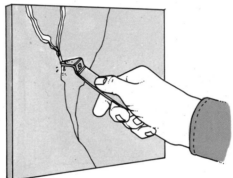 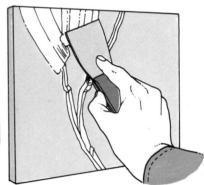

Fixing Plaster Holes

1. For small holes, daub in some patching compound and smooth with a putty knife. Larger holes require more effort and time. First, brush or scrape any loose plaster from between the lath strips and around the edges of the hole, then undercut the edges as described above. If lath strips are missing, wad up some newspaper and pack it in as tightly as possible. Make certain the area is dust free and dampen it with water or spot-spray with primer-sealer.

2. With a broad putty knife, press some plaster firmly against the edges and pack tightly into the lath, filling the hole to about ¼ inch from the surface. When the compound is tacky, score it with a nail or the edge of your putty knife. Let it dry, then moisten and repeat the process, filling the hole to within ⅛ inch of the wall. After sanding around the patch, apply a top coat level with the surrounding surface, sand again, and prime.

Matching the Surface

To hide your patch, try to match its final surface to that of the surrounding wall. Experiment with a sponge, a stiff brush, or a roller cover. Dampen the tool so it doesn't pull away the surface of your patch. Professionals sometimes put sand in patching plaster to match rough-textured surfaces.

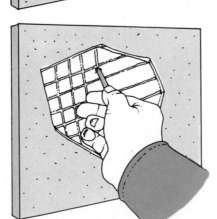 

Patching Wallboard

Wallboard is far less likely than plaster to develop cracks, but holes present a special problem: there's no backing to hold in your patching material. Small surface gouges can be filled with a sweep of your putty knife, but bigger jobs may need two or three layers.

1. Clear away any loose material, then spray the edges of the hole with fast-drying primer. Punch a hole through a piece of cardboard slightly larger than the hole and insert a knotted string. Push the cardboard through the hole, and pull it tight.

2. Apply fast-setting patching compound, pushing the material well into the hole so that it will ooze around the edges of the cardboard and bind it into place behind the wallboard. The patch should be about ¼ inch below the surface. In a few moments, release the string. Score the surface of the patch and cut the string close to the wall.

3. Top the patch with smooth-grain vinyl patching compound, using a 6-inch putty knife. When the surface is tacky, match it to the surrounding surface.

For large holes, use a utility knife to cut the damaged area into a beveled square or rectangle, with the widest edge on the outer surface of the wall. Cut a matching but slightly smaller square from wallboard scrap. Spot-prime and apply joint or patching compound around all edges, then push the patch into place about ⅛ inch inside the wall surface. Finish by skim-coating: dip your putty knife into water, then skim on a thin top coat of patching or joint compound.

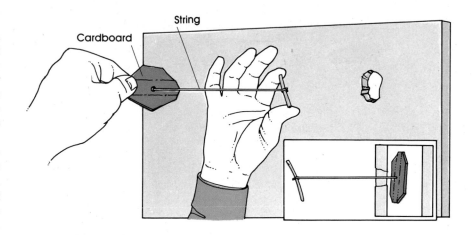

Cardboard String

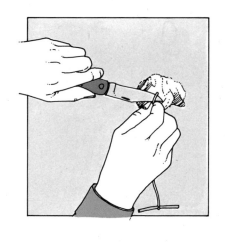

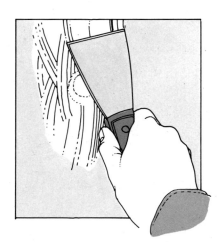

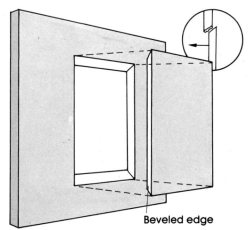

Beveled edge

Painting Over Wallpaper

There aren't many times when you'll want to paint over wallpaper. For one thing, your paint job is only as solid as the paper's adhesion to the wall; if moisture later weakens the paste, you've lost a lot of hard work. And some papers, such as flocked ones, are so bumpy that painting over them produces an unattractive surface. Before you decide to paint over paper, tug on a corner to see if it is "strippable"—nearly all vinyl coverings are. If

the paper is strippable, remove it. If the paper isn't strippable, you'll need to repair problem areas by gluing down loose spots and slitting air bubbles (see page 84). In areas where paper is badly torn or missing, flake off any peeling edges with a broad putty knife, feather in some patching compound, and sand lightly when dry. It's best to seal the entire surface with a good oil-based primer, especially if you'll be painting over a brightly colored pattern.

Repairing Ceilings

Ceiling cracks are usually caused by moisture intrusion or heat; temperature assaults the top of a room as fiercely as any area of your house. If the surface has actually split open and begun flaking, pick away as much plaster as you can with your fingers; then, using a putty knife, scrape at the surrounding area until you get to plaster that resists removal. Prime the exposed area and fill with patching plaster as for the final layer of wall repair (see page 36).

You might also want to try one of the flexible compounds developed in recent years. Used in combination with a fabriclike mesh, these compounds are especially suited to ceilings with widespread humping or bulging of the surface plaster or numerous fine cracks. Flexible compounds will not make the surface even, but they can disguise flaws and prevent hairline cracks from widening. They are amazingly easy to apply and have the ability to expand and contract, providing a surface capable of withstanding considerable shifts in underlying material. They cannot be sanded, which is not a severe drawback on rough-textured ceilings, but limits their use on walls, where patched areas generally must be smooth before painting. In some instances, with only a few minutes' work, flexible compounds can help you avoid a costly replastering job. Most of these materials can be applied as shown below.

1. Make certain the area is grease free, washing with a strong detergent if necessary. When the area is dry, brush it *lightly* to clear away dust or loose material, taking care to disturb the crack as little as possible. Using the applicator supplied by the manufacturer or a wide putty knife, scoop up some of the flexible compound (the smooth-grained variety is best for interior use) and spread it liberally along the length of the crack.

2. Cut fabric mesh material the length of the crack and imbed it in the compound. Smooth any wrinkles, applying enough pressure to press the fabric against the surface and fill the mesh. Allow the compound to dry.

3. Smooth a final coat of compound over the patch, spreading it lightly but thickly enough to cover the fabric. Feather the edges into the surrounding ceiling. When the material is tacky, tap it with the end of a brush or lightly pat it with a sponge to stipple the surface so it matches the surrounding area. Do not attempt to sand the patch.

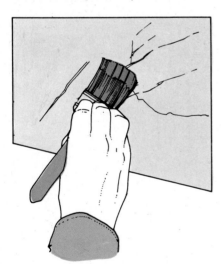

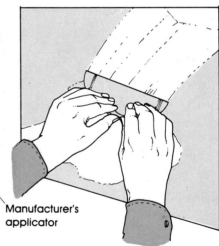

Manufacturer's applicator

Getting Rid of Mildew

Mildew is caused by excess moisture, usually in combination with warm temperatures and poor ventilation. It looks like splotchy dirt. If you're uncertain what you're dealing with, spot the surface with chlorine bleach. If the bleach removes the dirty spot, you've got mildew. This stubborn fungus has long been an enemy of upper walls and ceilings; painters once used paint fortified with tincture of mercury—a deadly poison—to combat it. Today, you can start by cleaning your wall with a formula recommended by the National Paint and Coatings Association: 1 quart chlorine bleach mixed with 3 quarts warm water. Wear rubber gloves to apply the mixture.

You can also buy a premixed commercial spray mildew remover. Scrub either solution vigorously into the surface. Rinse the surface thoroughly with water and allow to dry. Then use a paint containing an antimildew ingredient, or add a special fungicide (available from your paint store). The binders in both latex and oil-based paints can provide nutrients for mildew, so you should be certain that your primer contains a fungicide.

The best solution, of course, is to eliminate the conditions that cause mildew to flourish. You may not be able to control the temperature, but a good fan can improve your ventilation and a dehumidifier can lower your room's moisture.

PREPARATION: WOODWORK

Woodwork is generally the last thing you paint, but you should prepare trim along with the rest of the room. Most woodwork is already painted with some type of gloss finish. Because new paint will not stick to such a surface, you must roughen it before repainting. Similarly, previously stained woodwork should be sanded and primed before painting. New wood surfaces should be lightly sanded before priming and again before the finish coat. The following instructions will help you prepare all your wood trim.

Scraping

If old trim paint is badly checkered or peeling, you may need to scrape the entire area. Use a putty knife or straight-blade scraper for small areas and a pull scraper for larger areas. For major jobs, get a water-soluble gel remover, apply it according to instructions, and then lift the softened paint off with the scraper blade. Keep the blade as close to parallel to the surface as possible to avoid scarring the underlying surface. After scraping, sand as described below.

Filling Gouges and Dents

Brush out or sand the area to be filled. Then spray with a good sealing primer. Using a small putty knife, fill the gouge with fine-grained wood putty or patching compound. Don't use fast-setting compounds; their surfaces are too hard to sand. If the gouge is more than ⅛ inch deep, apply two layers of compound. Sand the patch, feathering the edges. Spray with primer.

Sanding

You should always sand areas where there are breaks between the old paint film and the underlying surface. You may have to sand the entire area or you may be able to spot-sand. Start with coarse sandpaper —60- to 80-grit —and move to progressively finer papers, ending with fine aluminum oxide paper. Work lengthwise along the molding or trim.

You can use a sanding block for most surfaces, but for smaller areas, just fold the paper in your hand. Power sanders are much faster, but disc sanders require skill. Use only those disc sanders that accept flat, adhesive-backed sanding sheets. Better yet, use an orbital sander.

Dust can ruin a paint job. After all sanding, wipe the surfaces with a tack cloth.

Deglossing

The repaired surfaces now need to be roughed up a little for painting. You can sand lightly, or apply a commercial deglossing agent. Avoid brands with ethyl alcohol; they emit strong odors and can make you nauseated or groggy. (You can also use a very strong solution of trisodium phosphate, but it leaves a film that you must rinse off.)

First, wipe the surface with a damp rag and let it dry. Then moisten a cloth with the deglossing compound and wipe it on with good strong strokes. Be careful that you use only a moderate amount; if you put too much on, it will leave a film, which defeats the purpose. Let it dry, and you're ready to paint.

Spray-prime before and after puttying

Protect window

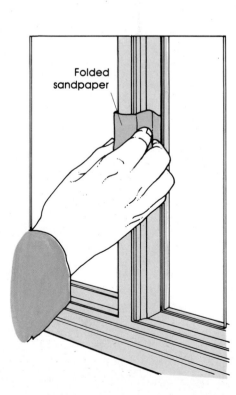

Folded sandpaper

PREPARATION: CLEANING & PICKING UP

The Last Cleanup

The final step in preparing to paint a room begins with an all-out vacuum and dusting attack on such demon dirt-hiding places as windows, door tops, baseboards, cabinets, and ceiling molding. Try to get it all; every bit of dirt you paint is a speck of paint that won't stick. When you're through, sponge off the area you're planning to paint with a heavy-duty household detergent (some dishwasher soaps that contain TSP can do an effective job). For especially greasy spots, use a rag soaked in thinner but be careful to extinguish pilot lights in any nearby gas stoves or heaters.

Picking Up

The painter's dream room is mostly empty. Before starting your paint job, prepare your room as shown in the drawing below. Remove as many of the room's furnishings as possible. Pull any remaining furniture into the center of the room and cover it with drop cloths. Remove draperies, curtains, and rods; switch and outlet plates (leave their screws in to prevent loss); and door hardware if doors are to be painted. Loosen the base plates of ceiling-mounted light fixtures, and use masking tape to protect window panes. It's also wise to mask electrical outlets and switches after removing their cover plates.

Patched areas

Switchplate cover removed

Furniture covered with plastic

Floor protected

Where Do I Start?

Follow this sequence when painting any room:

1. ceiling
2. walls
3. windows
4. doors and other woodwork
5. baseboards

Before painting either walls or ceilings, use a brush to "cut in" (see page 43) borders of up to 4 inches. Finish with a roller, overlapping brush marks. Start ceilings in a corner and work across the narrower dimension. Start walls in an upper corner and work in vertical sections. See pages 42–45 for brush and roller techniques.

PREPARATION: PAINT

If you begin your paint job soon after purchasing your paint, it should need only stirring. However, if you're using paint that has been stored for a while, stirring and, in many cases, thinning will be needed to produce a smooth, evenly blended paint that flows properly. With latex paints, it's probably better to stir with a paint stick than with the dealer's machine shaker; shaking can create fine air bubbles that show up as craters on your walls. And stirring can help you decide how much thinning is needed.

Boxing

"Boxing" is the way professionals stir. Boxing can be a good way to protect yourself against a color mismatch when you're using a number of cans of paint. Simply carry out the boxing process with two or more cans of paint.

1. Pour most of the thin top paint from the can into a separate pail. (Paint stores sell cheap disposable buckets that are excellent for stirring.)

2. Stir the thick paint in the bottom of the can until it is free of lumps and uniform in color.

3. Slowly pour the "thin" paint back into the can, stirring it into the heavier paint. Pour paint back and forth between pail and can until the color and consistency are uniform.

Thinning

If your brush is leaving furrows that don't blend, or the nap on your roller seems to be pulling the paint away from the wall, you probably need to do some thinning. Add an ounce of water or thinner, stir thoroughly, and brush the paint on the wall to test it. If it is still not right, continue thinning, adding an ounce at a time until the paint blends into an even film on the wall surface.

Exercise moderation in thinning: once you've gone too far, you may be stuck with a Hobson's choice between working with a runny, sagging product or going out and buying more paint to beef up what you've got. If you've thinned your paint and it still doesn't flow properly, talk to your dealer. You may be using the wrong brush or roller.

Straining

Air can cause a thick scum on oil-based paints. Don't try to mix the skin back into the paint. Instead, gently loosen the skin enough to pour the paint into a separate can. Use a discarded nylon stocking or cheesecloth as a strainer.

Draining

Paint often dribbles into the groove at the top of the can and thus prevents an airtight seal. You can buy a plastic lip-guard gadget, but a cheaper solution is simply to pound a few nail holes in the bottom of the groove.

TECHNIQUES: BRUSHES

Though rollers are now used to paint most walls and ceilings, brushes dominate when it comes to nearly everything else, including doors, molding, windows, baseboards, cabinets, and shelves, as well as unusually rough-textured walls. Brushes are also used to cut in border areas that are more difficult to cover with a roller. Probably the main reason for their popularity is that brushes spread paint more efficiently than any other painting tool. And what brushes sacrifice in speed (compared with a roller, for example), they more than make up in control.

The width of your brush generally depends on the surface being painted and your strength—a wide brush can become surprisingly heavy. Avoid using a brush wider than the surface being covered; you'll splay the bristles or, if you turn it on its side, distort the brush's shape. Use a trim brush, up to 2 inches wide, for straight work,

and a 1½-inch angled brush for window sashes. When using an angled brush, pull through your stroke with enough pressure that the tips of the bristles—never their sides—carry the paint. See pages 34–35 for more information on brushes and where to use them.

Holding a brush. There probably isn't a single "best way" to hold a paint brush, and in fact it's a good idea to shift your grip slightly while painting to avoid hand and arm fatigue. Most professional painters hold the handle lightly, as you might a hand of playing cards, with the thumb supporting the underside of the brush and the fingers guiding it from the top as they stroke down the wall. If you've got small hands or you're using a wide brush, wrap your fingers around the handle as if it were a tennis racquet. A small trim brush can be held like a pencil, between your thumb and your first and second fingers.

How to Paint With a Brush

Tip in. Dip the brush to no more than half its bristle length. Lift the brush straight up and slap it lightly against the inside of the pail. Don't draw the brush across the rim (you'll get clumpy bristles and flood the can's lip).

Lay on. With your brush at about a 45-degree angle to the surface, apply paint in long, light vertical strokes. On walls or ceilings, work in sections 3 feet square and slightly overlap previously painted areas. When painting woodwork, work from top to bottom on vertical trim, from left to right on horizontal moldings and baseboards. Whatever the surface, make sure the entire tip of the brush touches the surface.

Brush out. Next, spread the paint evenly over the surface. Using enough pressure to flex the bristles slightly, distribute it throughout the area. Use vertical strokes on walls and ceilings; follow the grain on wood trim. To keep paint from building up and causing lap marks, brush toward uncoated areas with long, even strokes.

Tip off. Feather the paint edges with light strokes using just the tips of the bristles. While still moving through the stroke, lift the brush away from the wall so that the paint blends with surrounding painted and unpainted areas in as thin a film as possible.

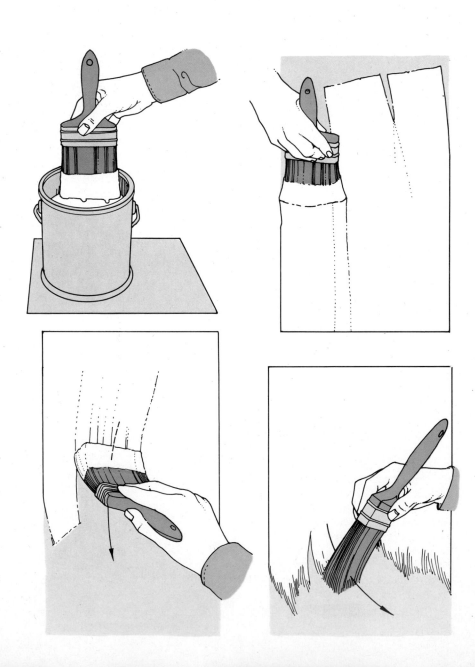

Keeping a Wet Edge

Lap marks, the bane of a good paint job, usually result from areas drying at different times. To avoid this problem, work so that you're always brushing into the section most recently painted, leaving a "wet edge" for the next area to be covered. When painting above doors or windows, work about halfway across, then complete from the other side. Feather the final strokes in a section (you'll be laying on a thicker load of paint to start the new one), and never stop painting in the middle of a section. Remember that most flat paints are more forgiving than glossy ones; they can often be successfully repainted even after they dry.

Wet edge

Masking Without Masking Tape

Many a professional painter who would sniff indignantly at using masking tape wouldn't be caught without a painting guide. These inexpensive metal or plastic shields are especially useful when painting baseboards or molding a different color than adjacent areas. (You'd still better use tape on window panes, however.) Simply hold the shield in one hand and your brush in the other, then paint your way across the woodwork. To avoid smearing, be sure to wipe the shield as you go.

Another possibility, especially useful if you are painting only the trim in a wallpapered room, is to use special light-adhering paper tape, available from your dealer in 3- to 12-inch-wide rolls.

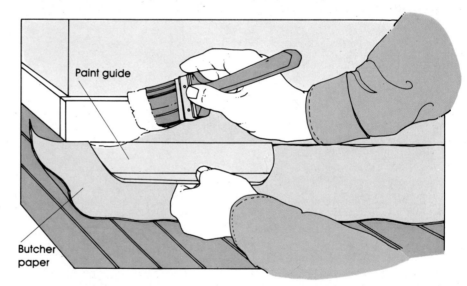

Paint guide

Butcher paper

Cutting In

Before you paint a wall or ceiling with a roller, paint a brush-width strip around all the edges of the section you're working on, wherever it meets a ceiling, molding, wall, or baseboard. Hold the brush as parallel as possible to the wall. Daub off any overload on the unpainted flat area; paint in long, even strokes. If you've got large hands and good control, you can use a 4-inch brush for faster coverage; most painters, however, opt for smaller brushes.

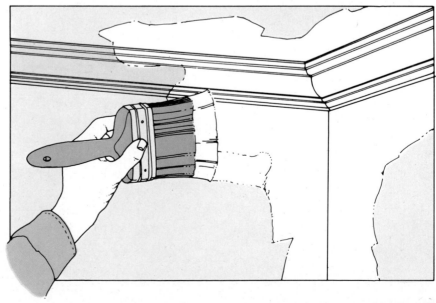

TECHNIQUES: ROLLERS & SPREADER PADS

Rollers are the preferred tool for applying paint to walls and ceilings. Rollers do have drawbacks; they use more paint than brushes and are sometimes not as effective in covering highly irregular surfaces. In fact, there was a time when professional painters frowned on rollers. But because rollers are fast and easy to use, those doubts have long since vanished. When it comes to large, flat surfaces at least, the roller is king.

How to Use a Roller

To remove lint as well as to prime the roller's surface for paint, dampen the roller with water (if you're using latex paint) or thinner (if you're using oil-based paint), then run it over a clean towel until it is dry. Roll it back and forth over the raised pattern of the tray until the paint spreads evenly and deeply into the nap, not just on the surface (a bucket grid helps with this). If the paint spills off the roller when you lift it, it's overloaded: roll it over the tray or grid again to squeeze off excess.

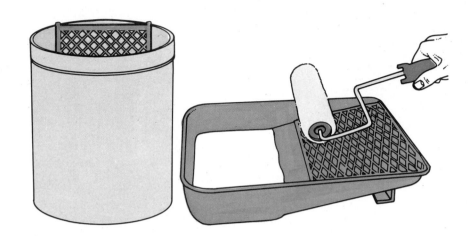

How to Paint a Ceiling

Ceilings should be the first area you paint in a room. Wear a cap or scarf and old clothes to protect yourself from drips. To spread as much paint as possible, choose a roller at least 9 inches wide, with a ½-inch to ¾-inch nap. Attach an extension to your roller. If necessary, rig a scaffold using a plank —at least 2 inches thick and 12 inches wide—on ladders or sawhorses or a combination of the two. Be certain the setup is steady.

Plan your work so you'll be facing the light; you'll have an easier time seeing areas you've missed. Figure on painting in 3-foot squares, and begin in a corner, working across the narrowest dimension. Cut in each square before you roll it (see page 43), using a trim brush or small roller to paint a 2-inch strip along the ceiling where it meets the wall and around any objects such as light fixtures. Take care of these detail chores from a stepladder before setting up any scaffolding that would be more cumbersome to move. Roll in a zigzag pattern as shown on the opposite page, with the first stroke aimed away from you. Feather into the areas you've cut in.

How to Paint a Wall

1. To keep drips and spatters off freshly painted areas, begin at a corner near the ceiling and work down the wall. Spread your paint in a zigzag pattern, starting with an upward stroke to cut down on paint drips. Roll slowly (to avoid spatter) and with increasing pressure, to spread the load evenly.

2. Without removing the roller from the surface, spread the paint from the zigzag to unpainted areas with even, parallel strokes, taking care not to roll too fast.

3. Feather the paint with a series of light strokes into any previously painted areas, or onto adjacent unpainted areas, and finish by lifting the roller at the end of each stroke.

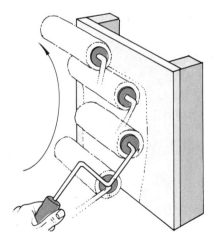

4. Reload and move on to the next section, rolling a vertical zigzag into the outer border of the area you've just completed. When you've repeated Steps 1 through 3, lightly roll the area between the two sections again—without reloading with paint—to avoid lap marks. Keep painting until you're through with the wall—don't stop in the middle.

Spreader Pads

Spreader and trim pads have become increasingly popular in recent years, primarily because they are faster than brushes and leave less surface texture than rollers. Even so, few professionals seem to use them, especially for putting paint on large surfaces; the widest spreader pads are still considerably smaller than a 9-inch roller. Moreover, pads require that you apply the paint with a single stroke; you can't pull the pad back across the paint as you would a brush. It's also harder to feather the edge of the paint with a pad than with either a brush or a roller. That can mean you run a greater risk of lap marks,.especially on walls.

However, pads do have the advantages of spattering and dripping less than either brushes or rollers. If you decide to use a pad, follow these steps.

1. Lightly moisten pad with thinner or water. Dry with cloth towels.

2. Dip spreader into paint (some pads are sold with a special tray that applies the paint from a cylinder), taking care not to soak the pad's foam backing. Lift the spreader straight up, allowing any excess paint to drip off.

3. Use long, straight strokes, all in the same direction. If the paint gushes out and runs down the wall, the pad has been overloaded.

4. Feather the edges by gradually decreasing pressure as you reach the edge of a section.

5. Pads that aren't disposable (the majority are) can be cleaned easily with thinner or water according to the manufacturer's instructions.

Painting From the Inside Out

When painting trim, it's best to work on horizontal surfaces before verticals and to follow the "inside–out" rule, working from inner sections to the outer portions. Use masking tape to protect individual window panes, but leave a hairline crack of exposed glass between the tape and the sash; that will allow a small amount of paint to provide a weather seal between glass and wood. Be sure to remove the tape as soon as the paint is dry.

For superior durability, use oil-based finishes for painting wood trim. For a wide section, you can roll oil-based paint on, then finish with a brush. With latex enamels, however, use only a brush.

Double-Hung Windows

Double-hung windows are the most common type. Start by removing all pulls, handles, and locks. Pour a couple of inches of paint into a small container.

1. Slide the inner window up in its slot to within a few inches of the top, and the outer window to within a few inches of the sill. Start with the outer window. Paint the mullions—first horizontal, then vertical—then the accessible parts of the sashes, horizontal before vertical (but don't paint the very bottom edge—that should match the exterior paint).

2. Slide the sashes back toward their normal positions, stopping short of closing. Paint the inner window as you did its mate, mullions before sashes, horizontal surfaces before vertical. Paint the top edge of the sash. Finish by painting the frame, first the top casing, then the sides, and finally the sill and its apron. When paint is tacky to the touch, replace hardware. Without closing them completely, move the sashes frequently while drying to prevent sticking. Though some professionals argue otherwise, it's probably best not to paint the jambs and parting bead at all; after the paint job is dry, lightly brush the jambs with a thin coat of penetrating sealer, then rub with a candle, shifting the windows so the wax covers the full length of the jamb.

Casement Windows

Casement windows are far easier to paint than double-hung windows. The only caution is to be sure not to paint any moving parts.

1. Remove hardware such as handles (but not hinges) and open the window.

Normal position   Reverse position for Step 1

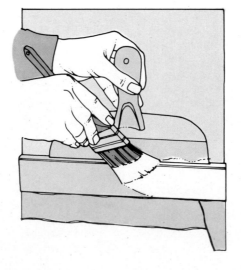

2. Paint any mullions, horizontals before verticals.

3. Paint the top, bottom, and inside edges of the sash, in that order.

4. Paint the frame, top first, then sides.

5. Paint the sill.

If your casements are aluminum, you probably don't want to paint them, though you may wish to apply a clear protective coating to combat special problems with pitting. If your casements are steel, however, they can be painted in much the same manner as wood windows. First sand with an emery cloth; its hard-cutting crystals are especially effective with metal. Prime with a primer meant for metal and then paint with a rust-resisting, oil-based paint formulated for metal.

Baseboards

Baseboards should be the last thing you paint in a room. An angled sash brush or trim brush can be used to paint the baseboard's top edge; use a painting guide to shield the wall as you go. (If you're only painting trim in a wallpapered room, mask the wallcovering with a light-holding paper tape as described on page 43.) Paint bottom edge next, protecting the floor. Paint the main body of the baseboard with a wide brush, or roll and then brush out. Other wood molding —chair rails and ceiling trim, for example—can be painted in much the same manner as baseboards.

Doors

The easiest way to paint a door is to take it off its hinges. Remove it by lightly hammering a nail against the bottom of the pin holding the bottom hinge, driving it out the top (the weight of the door could break the bottom hinge if you remove the top one first). Remove the pin from the top hinge, lift the door from its hinges, and prop it against a wall or lay it across two sawhorses. Do not remove the hinges. If using oil-based paint, you can speed things up by first laying on your coating with a roller, then spreading it with a brush, as described below; if you are using latex, use a brush for the whole process.

1. Using a roller, cover the door as well as you can. Work out from the middle, first up, then down. If the door is paneled, do the panels first.

2. *Immediately* after rolling, spread and even out the paint with a 2-inch trim brush, following the grain of the wood. If the door is paneled, begin with the panels, painting the molding that frames them first. "Pull out" paint from inside corners by working the brush into the corner and pulling it out and away from the surface.

3. The latch edge of the door should match the room it opens into; the hinge edge should match the room it opens away from. To reduce possible uptake of moisture, especially on doors that open to the outside, paint the bottom of the door (but not the top; a door sealed too tightly can warp). Paint the frame, working down from the top. Consult the illustration below to determine how much of the stop to paint.

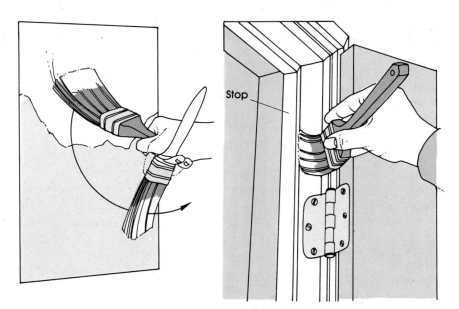

Cabinets

Follow the steps below if you're painting a cabinet:

1. Paint the inside back wall, using a trim brush, or a trim roller immediately followed by vertical brushing-out.
2. Paint the cabinet's inside top, or "ceiling."
3. Paint the bottoms of all the shelves, working from the top shelf down.
4. Paint the inside walls, working from the top down.
5. Paint the shelf tops and leading edges.
6. Paint the cabinet exterior, top to bottom, except the doors.
7. Paint the doors, interior side first (see above for painting doors).
8. With drawers standing on their backs, paint their front surfaces *only*. Do not paint any other part of the drawers or drawer openings inside the cabinet.

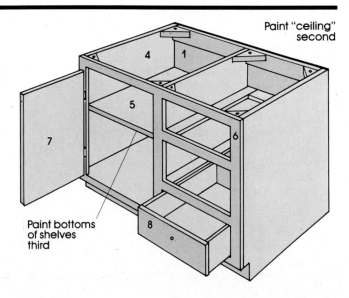

Paint "ceiling" second

Paint bottoms of shelves third

How to Paint Adjustable Louvered Shutters

1. Lay the shutter on bricks or blocks of wood, with the adjusting rod resting in the gap so that the slats can open freely. Open the louvers. Using a narrow trim brush and a slow-drying oil-based paint (to allow time to brush out drips), paint the inside edges of the frame.

2. Paint the inside edge of the adjusting rod. Starting at the top slat, paint the exposed surfaces of each louver, painting toward the center from the ends. Don't miss the front edges and the ends. If necessary, insert a stick between the slats to ensure access to their edges.

3. After the first side has dried, turn the shutter over and paint the rest of the slats. Paint the rest of the adjusting rod. Paint the frame, including edges. When it is dry, paint the other side of the frame.

For solid shutters and those with stationary louvers, follow the same inside-out procedure.

If you are painting only a few shutters, you might try aerosol spraying, but it can be expensive and may give an uneven finish. For airless spraying techniques, see the facing page.

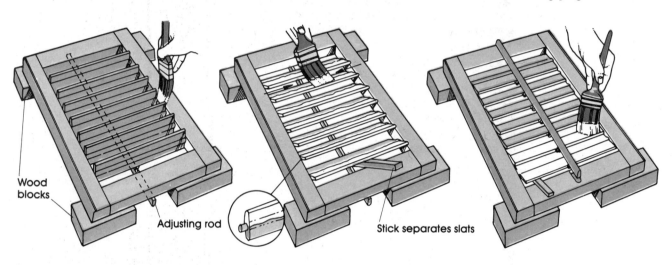

Wood blocks

Adjusting rod

Stick separates slats

Painting Masonry

Painting masonry requires special materials and techniques, most designed to deal with troublesome alkali in both concrete and mortar. To begin with, no new masonry should be painted until "uncured" particles of sand and cement have had time, usually about six months, to work themselves to the surface. When the masonry is ready, follow the sequence below.

Filling cracks and holes. Thick latex masonry paints will fill many hairline cracks on their own, but for larger flaws, pry out any loose material, wet the area, and repair with patching cement or mortar (use mortar for brick or block walls). Dampen the repair area and allow the patch to cure at least two weeks.

Cleaning the surface. Before painting any masonry wall, scrub it down with a wire brush and strong detergent. Remove any efflorescing salts—powdery deposits on the surface—by scrubbing with a mixture of muriatic acid and water using the following procedure:

☐ Wear rubber gloves and safety glasses.

☐ Pour 1 quart of muriatic acid into 3 quarts of water (*always add the acid to the water, never vice versa*).

☐ Apply the solution to the masonry with a scrub brush, then flush with water.

☐ Coat the wall with penetrating sealer (see below) as soon as possible—otherwise, moisture will pull more deposits to the surface.

Getting the right "tooth." If the surface is too slick for coatings to adhere, scrub it with the same muriatic acid bath described above. If the surface is too porous, paint on a "block filler," a special masonry primer designed to fill pores. If, however, the surface is covered with flaking paint or with whitewash or calcimine, you must remove the old finish first. Paint or whitewash may require sandblasting, a job better left to professionals. Calcimine washes off with a stiff brush, strong detergent, and water.

Painting. Use a long-nap (½ inch thick or more) roller or a thick-bristled, large brush to make sure the finish penetrates rough masonry textures. On floors, pour the paint directly on the surface, a little at a time, and roll it out. Most masonry work involves two coatings, a base coat and a finish coat. If moisture is present, the base coat must be a penetrating sealer, which will help lock in alkali while permitting the masonry to transmit water vapor so finish coatings will adhere. Another type of undercoat, known as a masonry surface conditioner, can help seal in and harden both unpainted masonry and masonry painted with aging, chalky finishes sometimes found in older buildings.

Latex masonry paint is the standard finish coat for most masonry, including brick. For concrete basement walls and stairs, however, special rubber-based paints are a good choice because of their moisture-proofing qualities. Epoxy paints (described on page 30) may be used on tiles.

TECHNIQUES: SPRAY PAINTING

Should You Use a Sprayer?

Sprayers can get paint into areas you'd have great difficulty reaching with a brush or roller, and they can lay paint evenly. But they require extra setup steps before you paint, are sometimes balky to operate, and, improperly handled, can pose a safety hazard (see below).

Small airless sprayers, the type most often used for interior work, generally hold 1 quart of latex or oil-based paint. They are widely available at tool rental shops.

A typical airless sprayer is powered by an electric piston-driven pump that propels pure liquid through the spraying tip. Follow these steps if you plan to use one.

1. Thin *and* strain the paint before use. You'll have to use extra solvent (mineral spirits) with most oil-based paints and extra water with most latex paints to get them to atomize well. The special viscosity gauges that come with some sprayers can be a help, but in most cases you'll have to thin by trial and error. Start thinning by about 10 percent. To avoid clogging, strain the paint through a commercially available filter or an old nylon, as described on page 41.

2. Test the sprayer on a large piece of cardboard. The paint should come out evenly, without spattering, and form an elliptical pattern, wide at the middle and tapering to the ends to avoid lap marks.

3. Because nearly all sprayers produce at least some overspray, be sure to mask or cover with drop cloths anything you *don't* want painted.

4. Hold the gun about 12 inches from the surface and move it horizontally, bending your spraying hand at the wrist to maintain the same painting distance through-

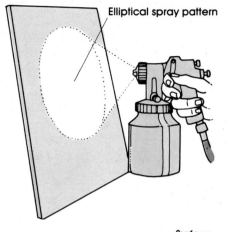

Elliptical spray pattern

Surface

12" 12" 12"

Bend wrist to keep nozzle
equal distance from surface

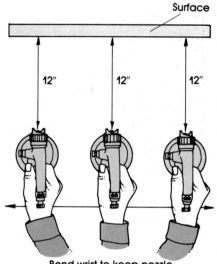

out your "stroke." If the sprayer and painting surface do not remain equidistant, the paint will be unevenly applied. If the gun is held too close to the surface, paint literally bounces off it, spattering outside the area you wish to cover and causing a sagging paint film and runs. If the gun is held too far away, not enough paint reaches the surface.

5. If your sprayer clogs, don't panic. *Unplug the sprayer's electric cord and release the pressure by pressing the trigger or pressure relief valve.* Usually sprayers clog when paint material gets stuck passing through the tip. Follow the manufacturer's directions to remove the tip and soak it in solvent. A toothbrush or piece of wire may help.

6. Always clean your spraying equipment thoroughly after each use. For the most thorough cleaning job, use lacquer thinner—a more powerful solvent than ordinary paint thinner—even when spraying latex paint. Carefully store the lacquer thinner, as described on page 55.

Sprayer Safety

Because they work at extremely high pressure—up to 3000 pounds per square inch—airless sprayers can pose a serious safety hazard at close range. Should you accidentally pull the trigger while touching the opening, you may be injected with paint. Such injuries may cause almost no pain or loss of blood but can result in severe tissue damage and blood poisoning. If you believe you have sustained such an injury—if you feel a sudden pinprick while operating a sprayer, for example—*seek emergency medical attention at once.*

When you acquire your sprayer, make certain it has a safety lock and guard to reduce chances of accidental discharge, as well as a protective shield to keep your fingers and other body parts away from the tip. Even these devices, however, cannot be considered foolproof; in addition, you should observe these precautions:

1. Never point the gun at anyone, including yourself.

2. Never try to clear the tip or take the sprayer apart until you've unplugged the sprayer from its electrical outlet and released the pressure by pressing the trigger or pressure relief valve.

3. Keep the sprayer locked away from children.

SPECIAL EFFECTS: GLAZE & MARBLING

The preceding pages have dealt with the materials, tools, and techniques required to give your interior a topflight conventional paint job. Having mastered this information, you may decide to probe the realm of the unconventional, where the art and science of paint combine to achieve decorative, sometimes spectacular, special effects.

Creating special effects with paint has a history centuries old; today, perhaps as a protest against the bland surroundings in which many of us work and live, special paint effects are enjoying a dramatic rebirth. Indeed, today's paint materials are being used to simulate Old World wood paneling, colorful Oriental floor rugs, shimmering moire silk wallcoverings, and even fine, hand-painted wallpaper, to name a few examples.

Sponges, rollers, and stencils. Some special effects with paint demand considerable skill and expertise; others are simple but require a willingness to experiment and practice with samples.

You can use a natural sponge to apply white paint over a light blue base coat and turn the walls in a small bathroom or child's room into a cloud-dappled sky. Or you can use a smooth-sided sponge to streak a dominant drapery or carpet color over a dining room or living room wall painted with a complementary base coat. Don't be afraid to experiment; as with many special paint effects, its inherent irregularities are sponge painting's greatest appeal.

Roller painting, or liquid wallpaper, as it is sometimes called, is another special effect within reach of the do-it-yourselfer. With this technique, the painter uses a roller with a design etched into its surface to paint a colored pattern over the wall's base coat. Ounces of paint are enough to do an entire wall and virtually any color can be used. An example of this technique is shown on page 23, where a pattern of brown flowers was rolled over a cream-colored wall. You may need to order these rollers through a local interior designer.

Stenciling is a special effect that has become a time-honored American tradition. Although it requires some inexpensive materials, it is nonetheless within the range of most serious home painters. See pages 52–53 for directions on how to do stenciling.

Painting with glaze. Glaze is one of the oldest and most popular materials used for special effects. Indeed, glazes were used to add depth and detail to Renaissance paintings and furniture. A thin, highly transparent coating, glaze can be used to mimic the appearance of rich leather, fabric, or aging parchment. Properly tinted, glaze can even create the look of wood grain.

Most glaze effects involve applying it over a base paint, then wiping some of the glaze off to produce a textured pattern, such as the crosshatch technique discussed at right. A satin effect can be created by pulling a metal paint comb in straight, overlapping strokes down a wall of tinted glaze. Your own hands (protected with rubber gloves) can finger-paint a spontaneous glaze design in a child's room.

Where to start. You can get more information about special paint effects from your dealer, art supply store, or interior designer. Check the adult course listings at your area's community college. Remember two rules of conventional painting, perhaps even more important when attempting special effects: Practice the technique thoroughly before putting it on your walls. And make certain that underlying surfaces are well prepared and clean.

Marbling

Marbling, among the most elegant of all painted finishes and the most difficult to achieve, should be attempted only by the adventurous. Surface preparation is critical, beginning with repair of all imperfections and application of at least three base coats of tinted enamel. Each coat must be sanded; then the surface is sealed with shellac and buffed with fine steel wool. The actual marbling begins with a thin coat of kerosene over which a paint and glaze mixture is applied. Using a sponge, a feather, and a dry brush, the artist creates a diagonal pattern of "continents" mixed with slender veins of color and then seals the wall with shellac or antiques it. For *faux* marble the colors are realistic; done well, it simulates marble with extraordinary accuracy. Fantasy marble, like the wall shown at right, employs a simpler technique for a let's-pretend effect. The marbling technique can be used on furniture as well as walls.

Crosshatching With Glaze

Because glaze effects can be planned only up to a point, you should experiment with large sample boards before painting your wall. Most glaze comes uncolored but can be tinted with artist's pigments or universal tints available from your paint dealer. Use an oil-based enamel as a base coat. Try different application tools such as rubber door mats, crumpled cheesecloth, worn paint brushes, and natural sponges.

Contrary to its name, glaze dries with a flat finish. For high gloss, apply a top coat of varnish, or subtly emphasize your pattern by using glaze over a shiny base coat.

You'll need about a quarter as much glaze as the amount of paint required to do the same room (see page 33). Be bold, but try and get the look you want the first time. You'll find glaze very difficult to retouch; rebrushing substantially increases its color intensity.

1. After applying a coat of primer-sealer, paint the wall with flat oil-based paint (use two coats for maximum color intensity). Paint trim, except edges closest to wall (they'll be painted last; see Step 3). Make a combing tool by cutting teeth in a rubber auto squeegee with a sharp razor blade or utility knife.

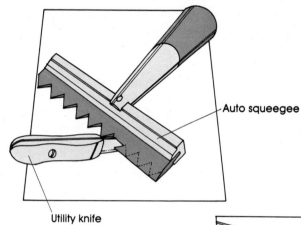

Auto squeegee

Utility knife

2. Using a roller to apply the glaze, start from an upper left-hand corner and work from the top of the wall down, in sections 3 feet square. Brush out with a wide (3- or 4-inch) brush (you may find an angled brush works best), feathering all edges. Take care to avoid overlaps and buildup, especially in corners and near ceilings—apply glaze as evenly as possible, use a "pull out" brush stroke in corners (see page 47), and feather each rolled section with a dry brush. Work on opposite walls; painting contiguous walls will cause glaze to gather in the corner from both sides. Avoiding bunching is especially important when you're using an absorbent material like cloth, paper, or a sponge to "blot" glaze onto a surface.

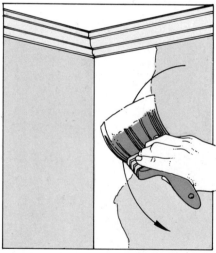

"Pulling out" from corner

3. Using the squeegee comb, rake the wall in horizontal strokes. Use the ceiling as a guide and make each run as long as possible. Then pull down the wall in vertical strokes. Don't worry about wavy lines; with glaze, perfection is not only unattainable, it would detract from the desired hand-painted look. Allow the glaze to dry overnight and finish with a glossy coat of marine varnish. Use an angled brush to paint edges of all trim.

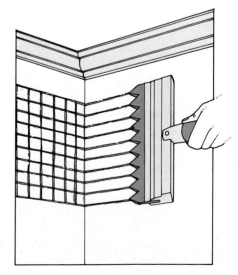

SPECIAL EFFECTS: STENCILING

A favorite of Early American home decorators, stenciling (from the French *estenceler*, "to cover with sparkles") is believed to have begun in ancient China, where designs were made with pinpricks rather than cutouts. In America, stenciling achieved its greatest popularity from the late eighteenth century through the mid-nineteenth century, when eagles, acorns, tulips, and grapevines —among other motifs—adorned walls, floors, and furniture from the Eastern Seaboard to the Midwest. Today stenciling, one of the easiest and most effective of special painted finishes, is enjoying a nationwide revival. You will need few materials—a stiff circular brush, heavy paper, and a sharp modeler's knife—and minimal artistic talent. The following steps show how to do a ceiling border stencil.

Choosing a design. Find a stencil design you like at an art supply store or make your own based on old designs (your library can help you locate pictures), or a pattern from your room's fabrics or wallcoverings. Be sure to choose an appropriate size stencil. Don't try to use a 6-inch-high stencil if the wall area you're planning to decorate includes spaces of less than 6 inches—between the top of a window frame and the ceiling molding, for example. And look at the scale of your design in relation to your room. A tiny pattern may be lost in a high-ceilinged room, and a large design may overwhelm a small room.

Be sure any "bridge" areas—nonpainted spaces that separate different parts of the design—are no narrower than ¼ inch (otherwise the stencil may break apart) and that the design itself is no closer than 1 inch from the paper's outside edge (so you won't smudge paint on your walls).

Choosing paint. You can use almost any kind of paint to stencil, though quick-drying finishes will reduce the risk of smears. Keep the paint's consistency on the thick side. For your first design, keep the color scheme simple, a single shade perhaps. With multicolor stencils, stick to strong, basic hues and do one color at a time, using masking tape to block openings that call for other colors. The parts you have painted will serve as register marks when you return for the next color. A palette can be a handy stenciling aid; make your own by covering a sheet of fiberboard with waxed paper.

The dining room shown below, in a restored Victorian home, displays a reproduction of vividly colored original stenciled borders.

Transferring the design. Tape your design over carbon transfer paper and your final stencil material (special heavy-duty stenciling paper is best). Transfer the design with a soft lead or wax pencil. To avoid any mistake when cutting, shade in the areas to be removed.

Cutting the stencil. Place the stencil on a stack of clean newspapers. Use a sharp modeler's knife and always cut toward you, turning the stenciling paper as needed (never leave your seat to follow the design). Take care to make clean, crisp cuts; since you'll only be making a single copy, burrs and tears will repeat through the entire design.

Positioning the stencil. Apply a light coat of spray-mount adhesive (a sticky aerosol available from photo dealers) to the back of your stencil and fasten it at a starting point near the ceiling with two pieces of masking tape, one on each side (since masking tape can lift the paint from your walls, take off some of its tackiness by first blotting it against your clothing). Plan your work carefully, dividing the distance to be covered along each wall by the width of the stencil; you'll quickly know whether to stretch the pattern out or squeeze it together so the repeat comes out even. Professionals find adjustments easiest if they work from opposite corners toward the center of the wall.

Applying paint. Load the stencil brush lightly by dipping it into the paint no more than ¼ inch, then pouncing it against newspapers to distribute the paint evenly. When lifted to the stencil plate, the brush should appear dry. An overloaded brush can seep paint under the plate and ruin your design. Using an up-and-down stippling motion and keeping the brush perpendicular to the plate, apply paint until the stencil openings are completely filled with color.

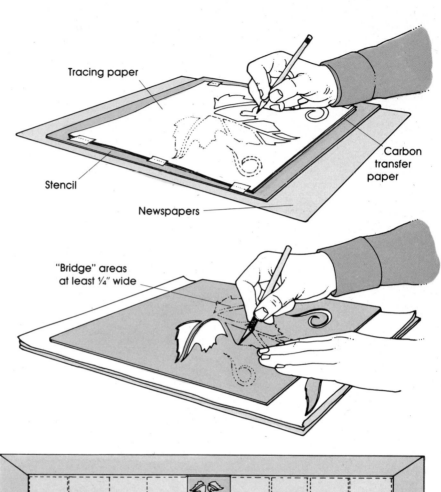

Tracing paper

Stencil

Newspapers

Carbon transfer paper

"Bridge" areas at least ¼" wide

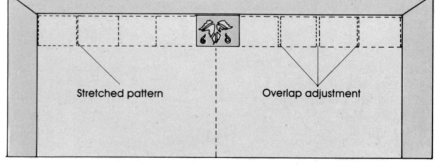

Stretched pattern

Overlap adjustment

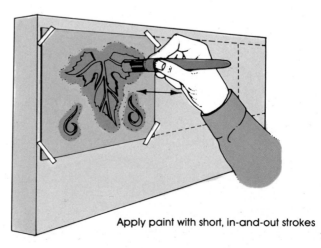

Apply paint with short, in-and-out strokes

CLEANUP & STORAGE

Proper cleaning and storage of your tools and paint can pay off for years to come. Paint kept in an airtight container, for example, will last indefinitely. Dried paint can be very difficult to remove from a brush or roller, so clean up as soon as possible after the job is done. And always match the solvent to the finish you used.

How to Clean a Brush

Whether you're using latex or oil-based paint, remove excess paint by scraping the brush against the sharp edge of a board.

Oil-based Paint

1. Pour some thinner or turpentine into a container and allow the brush to soak for a few minutes. Then work the solvent through the bristles and well into the heel. Repeat with fresh solvent. When paint no longer colors the solvent, shake the brush with a sharp, snapping motion. Wash the brush thoroughly in warm soap and water and rinse in running water. (Omit this step if your brush is made of natural bristles, which tend to swell in water.)

2. Pull a comb through the brush to free any tangled bristles. With the brush handle between the palms of your hands and the brush inside a large open container, spin off the excess solvent or water.

3. Wrap the brush in plain butcher paper, folding the paper around the brush in thirds and back over it to maintain the tapered shape of the bristles. Use a rubber band to hold the wrapping in place and store the brush either lying flat or hanging by the handle.

Latex Paint

Start by washing the brush thoroughly in warm soap and water, then continue with Steps 2 and 3.

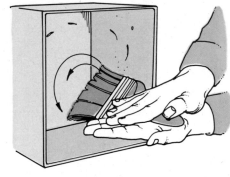
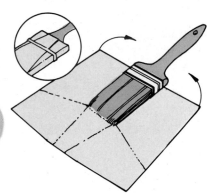

How to Clean a Roller
Latex Paint

1. Flush roller assembly thoroughly under a strong stream of water. Use a paint stick to dig paint out of the roller core. Slip off the roller cover and wash it in mild soap and water, working suds well into nap. Rinse and repeat until the rinse water runs clear.

2. Squeeze excess water from the cover, blot it with a clean cloth or toweling, and allow it to dry. Wrap the roller cover in plastic or butcher paper and store on its end (to avoid flattening the nap).
Note: the roller frame can be cleaned in the same manner, disassembling its parts as needed.

Oil-based Paint

Follow the steps given at left for latex paint, but soak the cover in solvent, working it into the nap, instead of washing with soap and water. Rinse the cover with fresh solvent and repeat the soaking and rinsing process until the solvent runs clear.

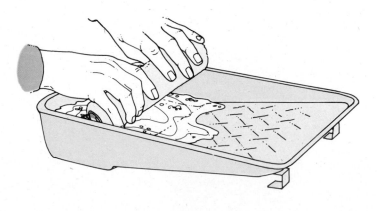
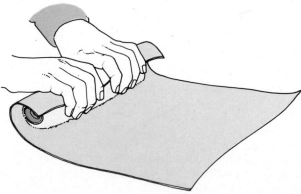

Storing Brushes or Rollers Temporarily

If your paint job lasts more than a day, you can set your brushes, pads, and rollers aside without going through the rigmarole of a full-scale cleanup. Before you start painting, drill holes through the necks of your brushes and at quitting time hang them from a wire in a coffee can containing paint thinner (for oil-based paint) or water (for latex); the liquid should completely cover the bristles. If you're painting with a roller, simply lay it in a pan of solvent or water deep enough to cover the nap, or wrap the cover tightly in plastic. This procedure also applies to pads.

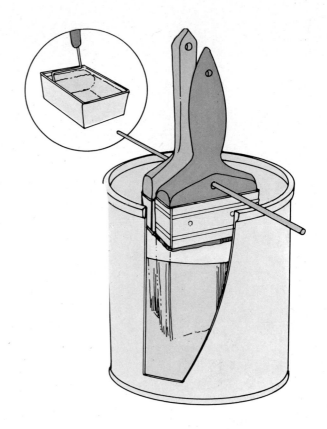

Disposal of Paint-Contaminated Liquids

Thinners and solvents contaminated with oil-based paint or varnish must be disposed of properly. Never pour these hazardous wastes down the drain or into a gutter or sewer. Nor should you put them in the garbage can for pickup—they can cause fires or explosions. Pour them into a container that can be tightly sealed, and label the container with its contents. Store in a cool place until you can dispose of it. Do not take these substances to a waste oil collection center. Many communities have disposal agencies for hazardous wastes; for information, contact your local waste exchange. Latex paint needs no special disposal precautions.

Storing Paint and Supplies

For your storage area, choose a cool, dry closet, shed, or locking cabinet. Wherever your storage space is located, make certain it is well away from radiators, heaters, or other sources of combustion; a few high shelves will help keep paint and thinner out of the hands of children. Transfer paint in half- to three-quarters-empty cans to smaller containers where there's less air to dry the paint out. (Another approach is to cut a piece of heavy waxed paper in the shape of the can lid. Place the paper inside the can so that it "floats" on top of the paint, keeping out air.) Wipe all can rims clean for an airtight seal and tap their lids on alternate sides with a hammer until secure. Label paint cans with masking tape and grease pencil (but not so their instructions and safety warnings are obscured). Include the color, the room in which the paint was used, and the date it was used. Push premixed patching compound flat in the can before closing. Scrape and clean putty knife blades to avoid staining future patches with rust or other substances. Hang brushes by their handles or store flat; in either case, make sure the bristles are wrapped as described on the opposite page. If you store a roller in a plastic bag, leave an end open to allow for air circulation. Fold clean, dry drop cloths and painting clothes and store on a shelf. If you're storing any materials containing solvent, however, wash them and allow them to dry before storing. Lock aerosols, lacquers, and other highly flammable substances in a metal cabinet away from sources of heat.

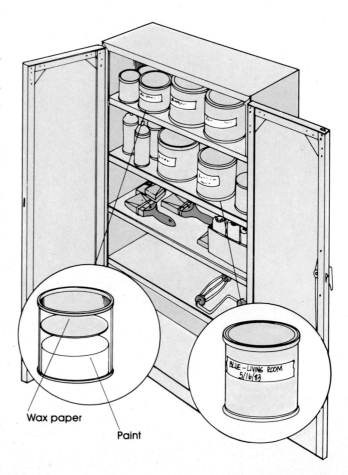

Wax paper

Paint

WALLPAPERING

This chapter helps you choose the
right wallcovering and hang it successfully.
You'll find step-by-step instructions for preparing
walls, planning placement, matching
patterns, and hanging paper anywhere.
Special section on hanging fabric, and
directions for natural wood finishes for trim.

The first wall "papers" were probably animal skins. Later came woven tapestries, hung on church and castle walls to keep out drafts. In 1481, Louis XI paid 24 francs for 50 rolls of blue paper decorated with angels 3 feet high, and the first flocked paper—made from powdered wool and metal sprinkled over a design painted in slow-drying varnish—was produced in England around 1680. By 1700, "painted paper" was being sold in Boston, although it was beyond the means of all but the wealthiest.

The advent of machine-printed papers in the nineteenth century began to bring wallpaper within the means of the less-than-wealthy. By the middle of the twentieth century, economical, high-speed reproduction techniques had further lowered the price barrier. At the same time, spurred by the rapid development of totally new materials, the types of wallcoverings expanded from traditional papers and fabrics to plastic laminates, all-vinyl coverings, and "natural" materials, such as cork, grasscloth, and hemp, on paper or cloth backing. Today, the choice of wallcoverings is limited only by the manufacturer's imagination and the consumer's budget.

Indeed, the range of wallcoverings is *so* broad that it is possible to spend weeks, even months, choosing. As a result, successful wallcovering demands careful planning. Study the opening section of this book for ideas and some of the basic principles that underlie effective use of color and pattern. Consider some of the following questions and make up a checklist like the "Paint and Wall-covering Shoppers' Guide" shown on page 25.

A child's bedroom becomes a leafy bower with the application of wallpaper in two-toned green. The curtains repeat the delicate, small-scale pattern, and the window shades are covered in a companion fabric. With white molding and an openwork bedspread to provide contrast to the monochromatic color scheme, the room is a fresh and inviting place.

☐ Where do you want to use wallcoverings? A home with wallpaper on every wall in every room could make your head spin. One way to vary your wall treatments is to use a mural (see page 86) on just a single wall.

☐ Are there special conditions in your home that affect your choice of wallcoverings? If walls are bumpy or corners and ceiling lines irregular, stay away from straight-line designs or shiny coverings such as foil and plastic film. If you can't replace an element such as unappealing carpet or kitchen tiles, wallpaper can serve as a "bridge" to a more attractive color; see page 7. Does your home have a strong architectural character that the pattern should harmonize with? It may call for large or small scale, formal or informal style, a contemporary or a period look.

☐ What sort of furniture do you have? For each furniture style there is a compatible style of paper. Modern furniture, for example, tends to look better with grass-cloths, geometrics, and abstracts.

☐ What can you spend on wallcoverings? Are you going to paper just one or two walls? Would it make more sense to choose better quality—a hand-screened paper, for example—and cut down on the quantity? Be sure when you figure your costs that you compare prices according to the area you must cover, not just the price per roll. Some bargain-priced imported papers can be considerably more expensive than an apparently costly one when their smaller total area of coverage is taken into account (see page 63).

☐ How well do you know your dealer? The range of coverings has become so broad that an informed salesperson can be indispensable in helping you make the selection best suited to your needs. But for you to get the most from your dealer, you need to do some work too. Think through the design considerations in Chapter 1 to narrow down your alternatives *before* you go to the store. Try to picture the entire room when looking at samples. Borrow the ones you like and put them in the room you're planning to redecorate. See how they look when it's sunny and at night under artificial light. Only when you're certain that the design you've chosen is right for your setting should you make your final purchase.

THE LANGUAGE OF WALLPAPER

Backtacking
A technique for mounting fabric wallcoverings in which the material is folded back over upholsterer's tape and stapled. See pages 90–91.

Bolt
The commercial package in which wallpaper is sold, usually consisting of two or more rolls.

Booking
The technique of folding pasted wallpaper strips face to face. See page 73.

Border
A narrow strip of wallcovering used around windows and doorways or along ceilings.

Butted seam
A seam in which wallpaper strips meet edge to edge, without overlapping.

Ceiling break
Where the top of a wall meets the ceiling.

Chair rail
A strip of decorative wall molding, about 30 inches above the floor, which can be used to separate various elements of decor, including paint and wallpaper. Chair rails, dados, cornices, and other architectural details can be simulated with wallpaper.

Color run
The dye lot or run number of a batch of wallpaper rolls printed at the same time. Because inks and background colors are apt to vary among printings, the number is printed on the paper; if you must order additional rolls of a paper, be sure to specify the color run number from your initial purchase.

Companion wallcoverings
Wallcoverings that have been designed and patterned to harmonize with one another. Some wallpapers have companion fabrics, too.

Cornice
The horizontal molding at the top of the wall, located at or near the ceiling break.

Cutting wheel
A tool for trimming wallpaper, consisting of a sharp wheel spinning on

the end of a handle. Another trimming tool is the razor knife, shown opposite.

Dado
The space on a wall between the top of the baseboard and the chair rail.

Embossed paper
Wallpaper whose design is raised, creating a pattern in relief, as opposed to the more conventional method of printing a pattern in ink on the paper's surface.

Enamel undercoat (oil-based)
A primer coating characterized by its high degree of "tooth." Because its greater porosity better absorbs the moisture from paste, professional wallcovering hangers generally prefer enamel undercoat to glossier primer-sealers.

Flocked paper
Wallpaper made by shaking crushed nylon or rayon onto a design made with slow-drying paint.

Lapped seam
A seam between two wallpaper strips created by overlapping the edges.

Lining paper
A plain paper, also known as blank stock, used under certain wallcoverings to provide a smooth surface and greater paste absorption.

Mural
A wallcovering in which a number of strips portray a single subject.

Pattern match
The alignment of the design on wallcovering strips that creates a continuous horizontal flow of pattern around the room. Patterns match either straight across or diagonally.

Pattern repeat
The number of vertical inches between identical parts in a wallcovering design.

Prepasted paper
A wallcovering that comes with adhesive already coated on its back.

Pretrimmed paper
A wallcovering whose selvage (see "Selvage") has been trimmed at the factory.

Plumb line
A weighted line used for establishing true vertical on a wall.

Railroading
Installing a wallcovering horizontally rather than the more customary vertical installation. Railroading is often used with nondirectional coverings above and below features such as windows, doors, and fireplaces.

Seam
The line formed by the edges of adjacent strips of wallcovering.

Seam roller
A tool that uses a hard rubber or wood roller to flatten the edges of wallcoverings. Seam rollers are not advised for embossed papers, flocks, and most textured wallcoverings such as grasscloths, corks, and hemp.

Selvage
A blank strip along the edge of wallpaper. Selvage must be trimmed before the paper can be hung, but many of today's papers are sold with selvages already removed.

Single roll
The basic unit used in pricing wallpaper. Most single rolls contain 36 square feet of wallcovering.

Sizing
A sealer and undercoating used with wallpaper.

Straightedge
A guide, made of magnesium or steel, used in trimming and cutting wallcoverings.

Strip
A single length of wallpaper that is trimmed to fit the distance between baseboard and ceiling.

Strippable paper
A wallcovering that can be removed simply by pulling it from the wall, without using chemical removers or steam.

Vinyl
A plastic wallpaper, usually backed with paper or cloth. Vinyl coverings should be distinguished from vinyl-*coated* coverings, which are simply paper treated with plastic.

TOOLS & MATERIALS

In wallpapering, as with any other task, having the right tools can make a critical difference both in doing a good job and in having the work progress smoothly. Keep in mind, however, that you won't have to buy everything. Many dealers rent or, in some cases, loan wallcovering tools and equipment.

Large scissors. For cutting strips.

Razor knife. For trimming strips on the wall.

9-inch-wide roller. For applying paste.

Seam roller. For flattening edges.

Plumb line. For determining true vertical.

Smoothing brush. For brushing paper flat against the wall.

Tape measure. For measuring and planning the job.

Pencil. For measuring and marking off strips.

Water tray. For applying water to prepasted paper.

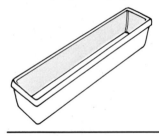

5-gallon buckets (2). For paste and clear water.

6-inch broad knife. For peeling old paper.

Trimming table. For cutting and pasting wallcoverings.

Sponge. For smoothing and wiping up excess paste.

Clamp. For securing paper at one end of the trimming table.

Carpenter's belt. For holding hand tools.

Stapler. For stapling fabric wallcoverings.

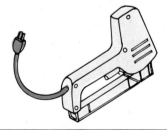

Upholsterer's tape. For back-tacking fabric wallcoverings.

Electric glue gun. For applying finish braid to fabric.

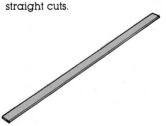

6-foot straightedge. For measuring paper and making straight cuts.

Stepladder. For working on ceilings, above doors and windows, etc.

TYPES OF WALLCOVERINGS

Cloth- and paper-backed vinyl; prepasted, trimmed, untrimmed, and hand-screened papers; flocks, foils, corks, and plastic films; silk, grasscloth, and other fabrics—they're all part of the increasingly complex world of wallcoverings. It may be helpful to think in terms of three broad categories—paper, which includes a number of materials that aren't paper at all; fabric; and special coverings, such as cork, hemp, and burlap. The distinguishing characteristics of each type are discussed on these three pages.

Paper Wallcoverings

Standard paper wallcoverings. Still the material of choice for most applications, paper displays an extraordinary diversity, encompassing both the cheapest and the most expensive coverings available. Machine-printed papers in the $5- to $15-per-roll range are available in widths generally ranging from 18 inches to 27 inches (the standard, easier-to-hang width). In nearly all cases, these papers come prepasted and pretrimmed. Hand-screened papers, on the other hand, can cost over $100 per roll. They are usually sold with intact selvages indicating how many separate color registrations have been used in their manufacture. In most cases, the more colors, the higher the price. Some standard papers are coated with a thin film of vinyl, but they are not the same as all-vinyl papers and cannot claim equal grease- and wear-resistance or washability.

All-vinyl wallcoverings. Scrubbable and damage- and stain-resistant, all-vinyl papers are simply the most durable wallcoverings made. They should be used wherever dirt and wear are prime considerations, such as in kitchens, bathrooms, hallways, and children's rooms. All-vinyl coverings are available in cloth- or paper-backed versions or as cloth impregnated with vinyl on a paper backing. They are smoother than vinyl-coated papers, on which the vinyl is thinner; when stressed, all-vinyl coverings tend to stretch rather than tear. They are usually moderately priced. Many professional hangers rank cloth-backed vinyls as the coverings easiest to work with. Because vinyl coverings lack porosity, mildew can develop in the underlying paste, so fungus-resistant vinyl adhesives must be used.

Foil wallcoverings. Foil papers are made of aluminum or, increasingly, of polyester films that look like metal, such as Mylar. Foils may be cloth- or paper-backed. Available in prepasted, standard-size rolls, they are among the most expensive and difficult to handle of wallcoverings. Nonetheless, foils can be a good choice for bathrooms or rooms that can benefit from this covering's unmatched ability to reflect light. Even the tiniest imperfections in a wall will be sharply highlighted by foil, however, so foils should be applied over lining paper (see page 66). The threat of mildew requires that you use fungus-resistant vinyl adhesives, never wheat paste. Similarly, it is not generally advisable to paste foil over previous layers of paper; trapped moisture might loosen the old paste. Avoid foils with selvage; trimming almost inevitably leaves creases and wrinkles. Finally, remember metallic (not plastic) foils conduct electricity, so *be careful around outlets, fixtures, and switches.*

Flocked and embossed coverings. Flocked papers aren't for hard-use areas, but few coverings can convey so much warmth and elegance in a formal living room, bedroom, or entryway. Their raised nylon or rayon patterns give the feeling and appearance of fine velvet, and they mix well with traditional furnishings. Flocks are available on standard paper, vinyl, or foil. Each should be hung with the appropriate adhesive, taking care to keep paste off the surface. Do not use a seam roller; instead pat down edges with a smoothing brush. Embossed papers have raised, nonfuzzy patterns that can add richness to your walls, mimicking the old-fashioned look of pressed tin, for example. They should be handled and hung in the same way as flocks. It is virtually impossible to hang new coverings over flocks, foils, and embossed paper, so proper priming and sizing are essential to ease removal later.

Murals. Murals are available on foil, paper, or vinyl backings. They may be scenes from nature—countryside or a stand of redwoods, perhaps—or skillful illusions such as a wall of bookcases that appear to be real. Murals need superb surface preparation to look their best; lining paper can be a big help.

Fabric Wallcoverings

Designer fabrics. These wallcoverings may be woven or nonwoven (the threads are directly laminated to a backing) and are sold through interior design shops in paper-backed, vinyl-backed, and unbacked yardage and rolls. Fabrics are available in widths roughly twice the size of typical 27-inch-wide wallpaper rolls. In general, paper-backed fabrics are preferred because they are easier to hang and because paper backing improves stability of open-weave designs. It is also possible, using special lamination services available through your dealer, to create your own wallcovering by backing virtually any material with paper. In any case, backed fabric wallcovering is almost always expensive. Its cost, and the disastrous consequences of spattering it with adhesive, are good reasons for calling in a professional hanger if you plan on applying a fabric wallcovering with paste. For some easier approaches well suited to simpler, less costly fabrics, you may want to consider the stapling or shirred-on-the-rod techniques described on pages 90–93.

Yardage. Wool, cotton, silk, felt, linen, burlap—almost any fabric can be hung on a wall, sometimes at bargain rates. The material shown in the room on page 21, for example, is a sturdy two-ply muslin called "upholsterer's decking" that regularly sells for less than $1 per yard.

To lengthen its life and protect against stains, most yardage can be treated with a protective spray similar to that applied to raincoats, either before or after hanging (check with your fabric dealer).

Nondirectional fabrics are the easiest to work with; they can be "railroaded" over and under doors and windows and tucked around corners without worrying about pattern matches.

Patterned sheets. Sheets have long passed the time when they were simply colorless bed coverings. Designs by the fashion industry's biggest talents, copies of the work of great artists, even blown-up photos of jungle beasts and movie stars have helped transform ordinary sheeting into extraordinary fabrics. Best of all, patterned sheeting ranks among the cheapest fabric wallcovering around. Often sold with coordinates such as matching spreads and draperies, sheets are the leviathans of wallcovering; a single king-size sheet can cover 9 square feet of wall. Because their patterns are usually difficult to match, however, you should plan carefully before hanging patterned sheets. Sheets are especially suited to stapling; padding the wall first with polyester batting can give sheeting a softer, more elegant look and help deaden sound (see pages 90–91).

Wallcoverings Compared

Type	Cost	Ease of Application	Durability	Wash-ability	Comments
Standard paper	Low	Moderate to high	Moderate	Low	Widest range of wallcoverings available at low cost.
All-vinyl	Low to moderate	High	High	High	Some professionals think cloth-backed vinyl is the easiest wallcovering to hang.
Foil	Moderate to high	Low	High	High	Requires special care in handling. Can cause glare in sunlight.
Flocked (embossed)	High	Moderate	Moderate	Low	Embossed papers can be purchased in white and then painted to match decor.
Murals	High	Low	Moderate to high	Moderate to high	Effect depends on exact pattern matching; vinyl murals have the highest durability and washability.
Decorator fabrics	High	Low	Moderate	Moderate	Should be hung only by professional or very experienced amateur; spray-treat for best durability and washability.
Yardage	Low to moderate	Low to moderate	Moderate	Moderate	Spray-treat for best durability and washability.
Sheeting	Low	Low to moderate	Moderate	Moderate	Spray-treat for best durability and washability.

TYPES OF WALLCOVERINGS

Special Coverings

Picture your walls covered in a rich linen, grasscloth, burlap, or hemp. How about shiny pebbles? Such special covering materials can create exciting effects, providing you respect the lessons of design covered in Chapter 1. Special coverings are frequently used in rooms characterized by the intangibles discussed on pages 22–23 —drama, character, and style. You should be aware, however, that these coverings also have disadvantages. Poor washability makes some coverings unwise choices for areas such as children's rooms that get particularly heavy wear. Special coverings can also be troublesome to hang: they can be difficult to cut when wet, and seams often can't be rolled with a seam roller. Nonetheless, special coverings provide a unique option you may want to consider. A few possibilities are discussed below.

Cork veneer. The warm brown tones and variegated texture of cork are often appropriate for a den, recreation room, or family room. An alternative to thick all-cork paneling, cork veneer comes in sheets only hundredths of an inch thick, which are carefully shaved from cork planks and laminated onto plain or colored backing. Cork can be hung without regard for pattern matching. Cork veneer should be hung over lining paper (see page 66), and manufacturers often recommend that only one strip at a time be trimmed, pasted, and hung; soaking or pasting sheets in advance may cause the cork to separate from its backing.

Grasscloth. Grasscloth is more formal than cork. It's available in synthetic as well as natural materials, and comes in a wide range of colors, from neutrals to strong hues such as purple. Some grasscloth patterns run vertically, but other designs come in woven "crosshatch" patterns. Although lack of a distinct pattern reduces matching problems, roll-to-roll variations in color are almost inevitable. As a result, grasscloth manufacturers often recommend arranging cut strips before pasting and hanging to minimize color mismatches. Never paste, book, and set aside grasscloth coverings, however. Like cork veneer, grasscloth is usually laminated to paper and may separate from its backing. Burlap and hemp are similar to grasscloth in most respects.

Exotic materials. Felt, suedecloth, straw paper, animal hides, embossed and sparkling polyvinyl, linen, even pasted leaves—these are a few of the myriad commercially available materials that have found their way onto our walls. They're not for everyone, but carefully employed they create dramatic decorative effects. In some cases these unusual coverings can be as effective as fabric in disguising flaws in walls and boosting sound and heat insulation. There are some problems with using these materials, however. Many of them suffer from poor washability, and most should be hung over blank stock to prevent their separating from their backing. Many of these coverings are expensive—prices of more than $50 per single roll are common—and, because they are tricky to handle, they are probably best hung by professionals.

Estimating Needs

The best answer to the question, "How much wallpaper should I buy?" probably is, "A bit more than you think you need." Because manufacturer's dyes vary between lots, running out of paper can mean finishing a job with paper that is slightly—but noticeably—mismatched. Moreover, there's always the chance of damaging a strip or two in handling, as well as the possibility that unusual spaces such as dormers or stairway walls will call for more paper than you realize. Don't worry about getting stuck with paper you can't use. If you end up with unopened rolls, many dealers will allow you to return them; however, you may want to keep them in case you need to make repairs or want to paper something small like a wastebasket.

The easy way to figure your needs is to jot down the measurements of your room and take them to an expert —your wallcovering dealer. For your own estimate, measure the length around your room (wall + wall + wall + wall = perimeter) and multiply by the height from baseboard to ceiling break. Divide by 30 (most wallpaper rolls have 36 square feet; using a lower number allows for damage and waste) to determine the approximate number of single rolls. Subtract a roll for each pair of standard doors or double-width windows. Add a roll for unusual spaces or exceptionally long pattern repeats.

If the paper you've selected has a pattern repeat, you may want to make a more precise calculation of your papering needs as follows (pattern repeats are discussed in detail on page 71).

☐ Divide the wall height (in inches) by the length of the repeat (in inches) to determine the number of repeats per vertical strip.
☐ Round off to *the next highest even number*.
☐ Multiply the rounded number of repeats times the distance between the repeats and substitute this figure for the actual height of your walls to determine the required number of single rolls.

Thus, if you have an 8-foot (96-inch) wall and a 27-inch pattern repeat, the pattern repeats 3.4 times per strip. Round the repeats to the next highest number: 3.4 repeats = 4. Multiply by the distance between the repeats: $4 \times 27 = 108$ (9 feet). Substituting this figure for the actual wall height, consult the "Rolls at a Glance" chart at right to get the quantity you need.

Although single rolls usually total about 36 square feet in area, widths and lengths can vary considerably, depending on manufacturer and style. The main exceptions are so-called European rolls, which consist of approximately 28 square feet. When you estimate how many European rolls you need, plan on getting 22 square feet of usable wallcovering, subtracting 6 to allow for waste and repeats. Be sure you know if you're buying a European roll; most wallpaper is sold in packages called "bolts," containing two or more rolls, so you could be short several rolls per room. You should also keep these distinctions in mind when comparing prices to determine actual papering costs.

ESTIMATING NEEDS

How Much Paper Do I Need?

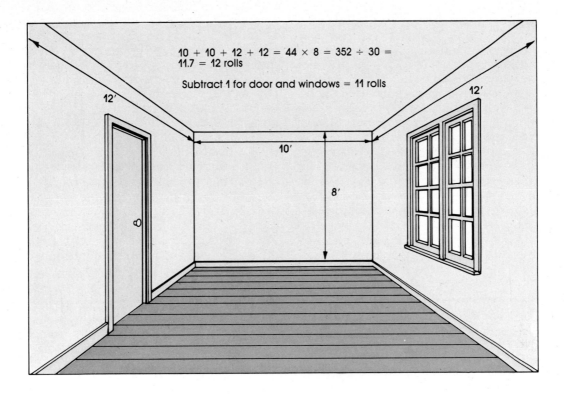

10 + 10 + 12 + 12 = 44 × 8 = 352 ÷ 30 = 11.7 = 12 rolls

Subtract 1 for door and windows = 11 rolls

12'

12'

10'

8'

Rolls at a Glance

The charts below give you a quick and easy way to calculate how much paper to buy. Use the formulas given on the opposite page. Using the corrected figure for your ceiling height to allow for pattern repeats, consult the chart for the number of rolls you need.

Single Standard Rolls

Distance around room in feet	Single rolls for room with			Single rolls for ceiling
	8-foot walls	9-foot walls	10-foot walls	
36	9	10	11	3
40	10	11	13	4
44	11	12	14	4
48	12	14	15	5
52	13	15	16	6
56	14	16	17	6
60	15	17	19	7
64	16	18	20	8
68	17	19	21	9
72	18	21	22	10

Single European Rolls

Distance around room in feet	Single rolls for room with			Single rolls for ceiling
	8-foot walls	9-foot walls	10-foot walls	
36	12	14	16	4
40	14	16	18	6
44	16	16	20	6
48	16	20	20	8
52	18	20	22	8
56	20	22	24	8
60	20	24	26	10
64	22	24	28	10
68	24	26	28	12
72	24	28	30	14

PREPARATION: WALLS

Preparing a wall for a subsequent wallcovering involves filling holes and cracks much as you do before a paint job (see pages 36–37). There are, however, two considerations unique to readying a room for wallcovering as opposed to painting. First, the wall itself should be as smooth as possible; any texture or roughness may show through. Second, the wall must be sealed so that it neither draws too much moisture from the paste (and hence away from the covering), nor permits alkalis or other corrosive elements to leach to the surface and discolor the covering from behind. Remember to finish painting any trim or ceiling or other areas before papering; trying to paint *after* you've papered is almost certain to lead to problems. When painting trim before wallpapering, carry a quarter-inch or so of paint onto the wall surface to mask any slight irregularities in your wallpaper cuts.

Getting ready. A clean, uncluttered area makes the best work space. Move whatever furniture you can to another room and shift the rest away from the walls.

Spread drop cloths over furniture (vinyl adhesives can be almost impossible to remove from fabric) and spread newspapers—or, better still, drop cloths—over the floor to guard against spattered water and paste. Now, survey the room. Take down drapes, blinds, curtains, pictures, and mirrors, as well as their rods, brackets, and hooks. To avoid redrilling, put a toothpick in any hole you'll want to use again; remove it when you paper the area and punch it back through before moving on to the next strip. Remove electrical switch and outlet cover plates and any light fixtures that will be in your way (see pages 82–83), being careful to shut off all power first. Keep an empty cardboard box handy for scraps and used razor blades. Finally, check yourself and your gear for cleanliness. Dirty hands can ruin an otherwise perfect job, especially one involving a light-colored wallcovering. Change cleaning water frequently and keep the tools you use for wallcovering clean and free of other materials, such as paint or patching compound.

Papering Over Paper

The quick answer to the frequent question of whether to paper over an old wallcovering is "Don't." If, nonetheless, papering over paper seems desirable (perhaps you're an apartment dweller for whom an extensive removal job just doesn't make sense), remember that the ultimate quality of your job depends on the condition of the underlying wall.

The general rule is that you can go ahead if the old paper still sticks tightly to the walls. One way pros tell the condition of preexisting paper is simply by listening closely while they run the tips of their fingers over the wall. If much of the area makes a crackling sound like breakfast cereal, the paper is too loose and should be removed. Another test is to flick the edges of a strip with your broad knife. If huge areas peel up easily, you should probably remove all the old paper; if not, scrape the paper back until you find an area that offers resistance, fill the scraped section with joint compound, and sand it smooth. Using white glue or wallpaper paste, glue down isolated corners or other small places that have come away from the wall. Remove any wax or grease stains with trisodium phosphate, and finish the entire wall with an oil-based enamel undercoat (see page 66) thinned according to label instructions.

If the existing wallcovering is vinyl, foil, or plastic film, papering over it may be tricky. First check to see if it is strippable (many such wall coverings are) by tugging at a corner (see opposite page). If it is not, sand the entire surface or use a commercial deglosser to roughen the surface enough for your paper to adhere (see page 39).

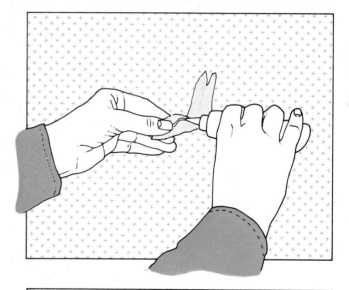

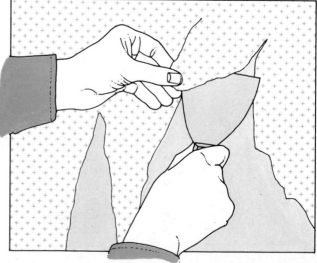

Strippable Paper

Many of today's papers are strippable—that is, they can just be pulled off the wall. Lift up a bottom corner with a scraper, then pull up and away from the wall. Remove all the paper, wash the walls with warm water, and scrape off the remaining softened glue with a broad knife. Rinse the walls with clear water and allow to dry.

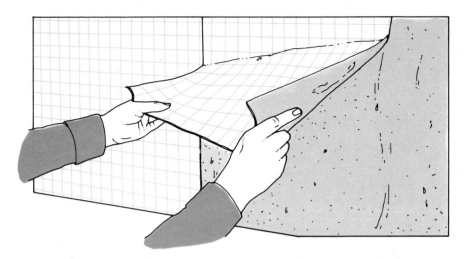

Chemical Remover

Chemical removers, available from your wallpaper dealer, soak paper off the wall by dissolving the underlying paste. You can purchase the remover ready-mixed or mix it with water. Be sure to follow any manufacturer's instructions about wearing protective clothing, including gloves or safety glasses. Then, using a broad knife and taking care not to scar the underlying wallboard or plaster, lift the paper away from the wall. Flush the walls with a TSP solution, rinse, and allow to dry. For three or more layers, you're probably going to need to steam your walls, as described below. Chemical removers are not effective in removing nonporous coverings, but such coverings are generally strippable or can be steamed loose as discussed below.

Removing Wallpaper With a Steamer

Wallpaper steamers, which can be rented from your dealer, use moist heat to soften the paste. The steam is pumped from an electrically heated tank through a hose to a hand-held perforated plate. When vapors from the plate loosen the adhesive, the paper can be lifted away from the wall with a broad knife as with a chemical remover. (With nonporous wallcoverings such as vinyl you must score the surface so that steam can reach the adhesive. To do this, use a special puncturing roller or tear the pa-

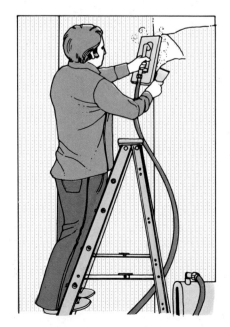

per's surface with a garden fork or coarse sandpaper.) Remove one strip at a time, beginning at the top of each strip and working down, allowing time for the steam to penetrate the paper and loosen the paste.

Note: when paper has been pasted to unprimed wallboard, neither steaming nor chemical removers will work. One approach to such a situation is to strip the paper off with wall scrapers. This is, however, a difficult, time-consuming proposition at best. A better alternative is to seal the surface with an oil-based primer and paper over it.

PREPARATION: WALLS

Patching and Smoothing

A good papering job requires that you fill in holes and cracks just as you would before painting (see pages 36–37), though you needn't be quite as concerned with matching the surrounding surface. The overall smoothness of the underlying wall, however, is of critical importance, since it is almost impossible to disguise an uneven texture. Deeply textured wallboard or plaster and rough or paneled wood should be leveled with joint compound, lightly sanded, and primed with an oil-based undercoat (see below).

Priming

Thoroughly sealing the wall can help your paper adhere by reducing the wall's capacity to absorb moisture from the paste. Walls painted with a flat oil-based paint need only cleaning and sizing; shiny oil-based finishes should be treated with a deglosser or strong TSP solution (see page 39). Otherwise—for unpainted plaster or wallboard, or for a latex-coated surface—apply an oil-based primer before papering. If in doubt, prime the wall. New plaster walls may have alkali "hot spots," so the primer should be followed by an enamel undercoat. Patched areas will benefit from the same treatment; at least spot-prime them. If pink "hot spots" still show up when you apply sizing, neutralize them with a solution of two parts water and one part 28-percent acetic acid (available from most photo dealers). Wear rubber gloves and resize the area after the pinkish color has faded.

Sizing

Though some professionals skip sizing, you're probably better off to do it. Besides further sealing the wall, sizing provides a tacky surface that can ease the job of hanging, especially with heavier, hard-to-handle papers. Because it provides an extra, easily removed layer between paste and wall, sizing can also facilitate later removal of the paper.

You can make your own sizing with wallpaper paste (choose a vinyl paste for greater mildew resistance) mixed to manufacturer's specifications, or buy specially prepared powdered or liquid sizing. On especially porous walls apply two coats or—if you're preparing your own sizing—a thicker mixture. Cover the entire wall and allow sizing to dry completely before papering.

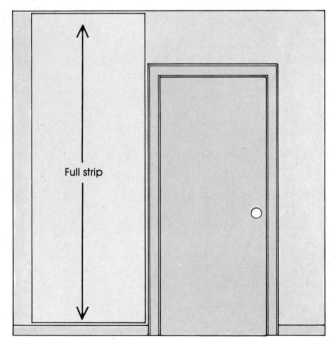

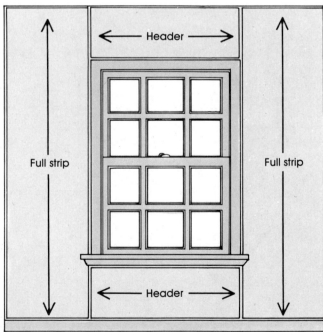

Lining Paper

Lining paper, or "blank stock," is inexpensive, unpatterned paper required as a preparatory step before hanging certain wallcoverings—foils, plastic films, and silk, for example—that could otherwise separate from their backing when wet. Lining paper's superabsorbency prevents such problems and can help hide small bumps, cracks, and indentations that would mar the appearance of special finish papers. Hang lining paper in full strips, leaving about ⅛ inch between the edge of the lining paper and baseboards, ceiling molding, and window and door frames. You can dispense with plumb lines, as well as the need to fit strips around windows, doors, or obstacles (separate strips of lining paper can be used).

Use "headers" (horizontal pieces) above and below windows.

PREPARATION: SETUP & SAFETY

Wallpapering means handling bulky strips of paper, messy paste, and unfamiliar tools and equipment. You can avoid many difficulties by setting up an efficient work place with your tools and materials conveniently at hand. The illustration below shows what a well-organized work space looks like. Its centerpiece is a 6-foot-long, 24-inch-wide trimming table, which you can rent from your wallpaper dealer. A two-pocket cloth carpenter's apron, which costs less than $5 at most hardware stores, can be a boon for keeping track of measuring tape, plumb bobs, seam rollers, and other small tools. Remember, too, to have an extra bucket for clear water and a plentiful supply of single-edged, commercial-grade razor blades.

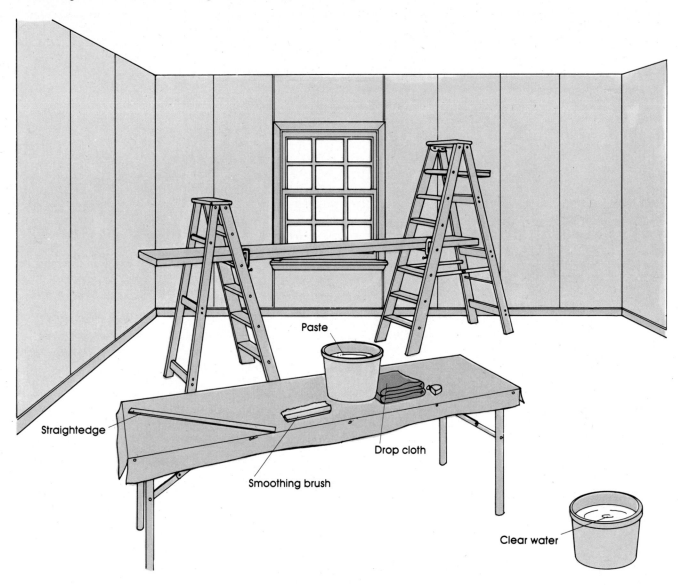

Paste

Straightedge

Drop cloth

Smoothing brush

Clear water

Wallpapering Safely

There are three main hazards in wallpapering: scaffolds and ladders, electrical fixtures, and razor blades.

Scaffolds and ladders. See page 81 on setting up a scaffold, and follow the safety precautions that are given on page 29.

Electrical fixtures. Shut off the electricity if you must remove any lighting fixtures. Once you have removed the covers over outlets and switches, avoid contact with exposed wires. Take care when cutting "blind" through paper over the unprotected openings, especially if you're using a metal-handled knife. Avoid touching chemical solutions, water, or wet brushes or sponges to uncovered outlets and switches.

Razor blades. Handle with care. Use only single-edged, commercial-grade blades (available from your dealer or hardware store). To avoid tearing paper, you should change blades with every cut you make; figure on using 2 dozen or more blades per room. Use a razor knife, shown in "Tools & Materials" on page 59, and have a safe receptacle handy for used blades.

PREPARATION: LATERAL PLACEMENT

Applying wallpaper involves calculating placement both laterally—the arrangement of the strips side to side—and vertically—adjusting the pattern from top to bottom on the wall. By carefully measuring and lightly marking off the width of every strip with a pencil, you can plan exactly where each piece of paper will actually go on the wall. If your task calls for papering more than one room, start in a room with large, unbroken walls that can be covered with full-size strips rather than one that will require more cuts per strip.

Where to Start

There's little likelihood that the distance around your room is exactly divisible by the width of your wallpaper, so if you're papering all four walls you're almost certain to wind up with a mismatch, a point at which you can't match the edges of two strips. The trick is to put the mismatch in the least noticeable spot; how well you succeed depends to a great extent on where you place your first strip of wallpaper. The discussion that follows will help you decide the placement of that first strip, depending on the features of your particular room (rooms with recessed windows, however, are a special case; see page 79 if your room has such windows).

Neutral patterns. Where you start is bound to be a highly individual decision, based largely on the architecture of your particular room and the design of your wallpaper. If, for instance, you have chosen a so-called neutral or nondirectional pattern, and the walls in your room are not broken up by features such as windows or fireplaces, a good place to begin papering would be an inconspicuous corner, behind or beside a door, perhaps. That way you can continue papering clockwise in full-width strips around the room, and the final "stop point" mismatch will be little noticed.

Focal point. In most cases, however, you'll want to paste your first strip where it gets the most attention—on the focal point wall. As discussed in Chapter 1, the focal point wall is the first wall you see when you enter the room. If there is more than one entry point, it is the first wall you see following the normal traffic pattern.

There are exceptions: some rooms—crowded kitchens and bathrooms, for example—lack an easily identifiable focal point wall. In other rooms, the focal point—the first thing you see on entering—is a corner rather than a wall. In such instances, you'll have to use your own best judgment about where to start. In a room with a focal point corner, for example, you could begin papering on either wall adjacent to the corner, but if one wall has a picture window, your best choice might be to start there.

Working from the center. Most of the time, you'll begin hanging paper at the center of a focal point wall and work out in full-width strips toward the corners, where any mismatch will most likely occur. Starting at the center ensures the paper's edges will match at the point most people are apt to look at when entering the room. But even this rule should be kept flexible. You might have to work out from the center of two adjacent walls, if, for example, one wall contained a window and the other a fireplace. In the end, however, the goal is the same: to make the most attractive presentation of the paper's design.

Planning. Regardless of your exact starting point, the most important part of any sequence for hanging wallpaper is planning ahead. You should know before you begin where each strip of paper will go and where any mismatch will occur. Before cutting even one piece of paper, get out your pencil and tape or yardstick and mark off the layout of your paper around the room. Remeasure and then measure again. Only when you are certain where each strip goes are you ready to start hanging paper.

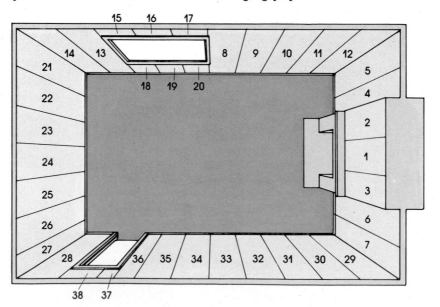

Paper sequence starting with focal point above fireplace

Centering on a Wall

If your focal point wall has no windows, measure off and lightly mark an X at the center of the wall. The X marks either the edge or the center of the strip, depending on what happens at the corners, particularly at prominent corners.

You don't want the last strip next to the corner to be narrower than 6 inches. Tentatively let the X mark the edge of the first strip and mark off the succeeding strips to the corner. If the distance between the last full width and the corner is more than 6 inches, center the seam; that is, paper as you've marked the wall, with the seam in the middle. If the distance between the paper and the corner is 6 inches or less, center the strip: re-mark the wall so that the center of the first strip of paper will fall on the X.

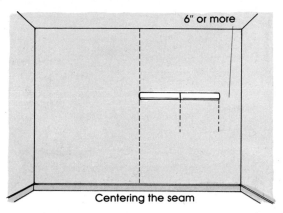

Centering the seam

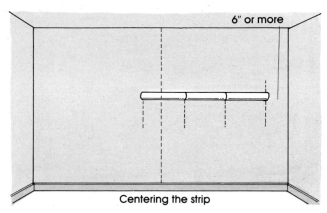

Centering the strip

Centering Between Two Windows

For a wall with windows, follow the directions above to mark the wall. If you wind up with more than 6 inches in the corner, center the seam. If you wind up with less than 6 inches in the corner, center the strip, *unless* that will leave unattractively narrow strips on either side of the windows. In that case, center the seam and let the corners fall where they will.

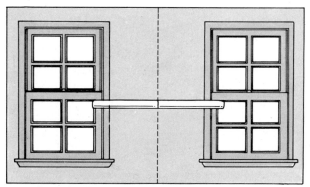

Centering the seam on a wall with two windows

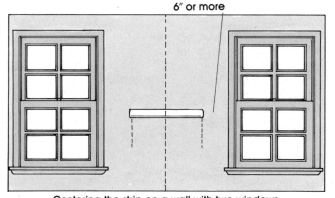

Centering the strip on a wall with two windows

Centering Over a Picture Window or Fireplace

Above a picture window or fireplace, the same criteria apply. You want to avoid strips narrower than 6 inches, but if you will inevitably have them either in the corner or next to the window or fireplace, put them in the corner.

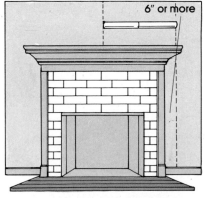

Centering the seam over a fireplace

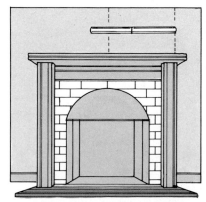

Centering the strip over a fireplace

PREPARATION: LATERAL PLACEMENT

Ending Auspiciously

Usually the shape of a room makes it almost inevitable that when the final strip meets the first one the pattern will not match. Sometimes, however, the room will offer "stop points" at which the mismatch will be hard to detect.

Wall break. If there's a complete break in the surface being papered—floor-to-ceiling windows or paneling perhaps—there need be no mismatch at all. See page 68 on preplanning the sequence of your wallpaper layout.

Corners. Corners formed by the short protruding walls of a built-in cabinet, bookcase, or fireplace are one of the least seen areas of a room and an almost perfect hiding place for your finish point.

Above a door. A traditional finish point for many wallpaper jobs is the little-noticed strip above an entry door, on the side closest to a corner.

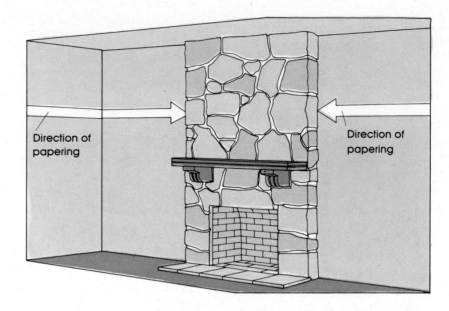

Direction of papering

Direction of papering

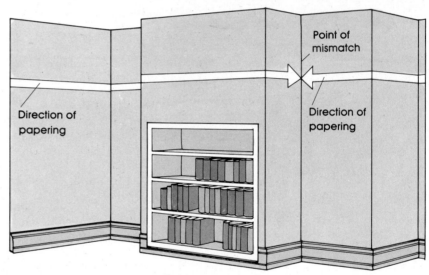

Point of mismatch

Direction of papering

Direction of papering

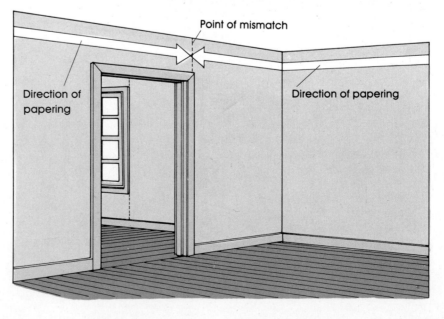

Point of mismatch

Direction of papering

Direction of papering

Besides proper arrangement of paper across a wall, you'll need to consider the vertical placement of whatever design you choose, primarily to make certain the wallpaper strips match at their edges. Before cutting even a single strip of wallpaper, lay two rolls out on your table and check the pattern match. Basically, there are just two varieties of patterns: straight-match designs, which line up horizontally, and drop-match patterns, which repeat diagonally in alternating strips. Both are discussed below. In general, straight-match designs and smaller pattern repeats are easiest to work with, especially for inexperienced hangers. Note: some manufacturers stamp the type of match on the back of the paper.

Straight-match Patterns

Straight-match patterns shouldn't present much of a problem beyond simple alignment at the edges. The same design repeats straight across, from strip to strip, at the same distance from the ceiling.

Drop-match Patterns

In drop-match patterns, the matching points are on alternate lines of the design, creating a diagonal pattern that carries the design beyond the width of a single strip. If you're working with a drop-match pattern, you may be able to reduce waste by cutting from two rolls at once or alternating the strips you use from a single roll (see below). Due to the extra paper needed for an exact match, drop patterns generally require one or two more strips to cover a room than would a straight-across match.

How to Calculate a Pattern Repeat

If a paper has a vertical pattern repeat, that is, if its design elements repeat themselves lengthwise, you'll need to take this into account when measuring and cutting

strips. The size of a pattern repeat can range from 1 or 2 inches to 2 feet or more. Generally, designs with smaller vertical repeats are easier to work with and involve less waste than larger patterns. That isn't always true, however. If, for example, your paper has a 27-inch repeat, and the area you're covering, including 2-inch top and bottom allowances, comes to 9 feet, the paper would repeat exactly four times in the space and there would be no waste. To calculate the number of repeats, measure the wall space (i.e., from ceiling molding to baseboard) you'll be covering, add 2 inches top and bottom, and divide by the number of inches between repeats in your paper. Thus:

$$\frac{\text{Wall Height (inches)} + \text{Allowance (4 inches)}}{\text{Pattern Repeat (inches)}}$$
$$= \text{Number of Repeats per Strip}$$

Scale and Proportion

Because lower parts of the wall are often obscured by furniture, the most critical visual elements of the pattern usually appear near the ceiling. If your walls are out of plumb, and many are, placing a prominent part of the wallpaper design at the ceiling break will make the uneven architecture even more noticeable. That's why professional hangers usually plan ahead so a relatively open area (between pattern elements) is placed at the ceiling break. In any event, avoid trying to make a pattern look straight by lining it up with the ceiling. That's a surefire way to throw your paper out of alignment. If your walls are perfectly aligned and you want a given design element to be located the same distance from the ceiling all around the room, snap a horizontal chalk line where the desired part of the pattern should appear. Use the line as a guide when planning where to cut your strips.

Cutting Strips

Many of your questions about pattern matches and repeats will resolve themselves in the cutting process, described below. Before wielding your scissors, however, double-check your paper for flaws and mismatched run numbers. Most dealers will accept the return of a defective roll, but only if it hasn't been cut.

1. Unroll a length of wallpaper equal to the vertical area you'll be covering plus a foot or so. Hold the strip against the wall and adjust it according to the way you want the pattern to appear at the ceiling. (Remember that it's best to place a less interesting part of the design at the break.)

2. With the paper still against the wall, lightly mark ceiling and baseboard lines with a pencil. Take the roll to your trimming

table and, adding 2 inches to the ceiling and baseboard pencil lines, cut the first strip with scissors.

3. For the second strip, roll out equal lengths of paper from the same roll and from another one. Laying the first strip beside them in turn, match the patterns and cut the second strip from the roll that wastes the least paper. Switching between rolls may save paper. You'll have to experiment a bit to find out.

4. Stack the strips in order, with the first strip on top. Then, to make the paper easier to hang and handle, roll the strips in the opposite direction from the way they were in the package.

Until you're an old wallpaper hand, it's best not to cut too much paper ahead. Start with one or two strips at a time, and never cut more than the number of full strips required to reach the room's first door, window, or other papering obstacle.

Plumb Lines

It's essential that wallpaper be hung straight, of course, and you can't trust your eye or just align the paper with the corner or ceiling break—walls are often slightly out of alignment. You'll need to mark a plumb line before hanging the first piece of paper, and you should periodically recheck plumb, particularly after turning a corner. You can purchase a plumb bob, but it's easy to make your own with string, some colored chalk, and something to give it weight, such as a fishing line sinker or a pocket knife. Tie the weight on the string and rub the string with the chalk.

With a pushpin, hang your plumb line near the ceiling, about ¼ inch away from the pencil mark indicating the placement of your first strip; because chalk could show between strips, plumb lines should never coincide with wallpaper widths. Let the line hang almost to the floor and wait until it stops swinging. Pull the string tight and snap it against the wall like a rubber band. The chalk on the string will make a straight vertical line on the wall. It's a good idea to use your level as a check against your plumb line.

Plumbing with a level. A 36-inch carpenter's level can also give you a precise plumb line. Place the level flat against the wall, slightly ahead of the first strip. When both bubbles are centered, draw a line. Continue the full height of the wall.

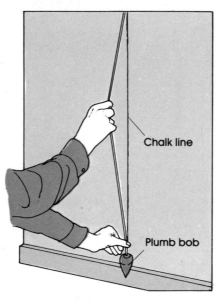

Chalk line

Plumb bob

Straightedge

Choosing and Mixing Paste

Wallpaper paste is available as either a wheat-based organic compound or a synthetic vinyl one. Either type is generally suitable for porous papers, but vinyl pastes are better for vinyl, foil, and plastic films, as well as for heavier wallcoverings that require a stronger bond. Paste strengtheners—condensed liquids added to paste to increase its adhesion—are also useful when hanging especially heavy papers and fabrics. Your best guide is to follow the paper manufacturer's instructions in selecting adhesives.

Vinyl compounds come premixed, but wheat paste can be made from a powdered formula that you mix with water. Because they lock in moisture and can trigger mildew formation in the organic adhesive, vinyl coverings should not be hung over paper originally applied with wheat paste. Be certain that any new paste you buy—whether vinyl or wheat-based—is mildew-resistant.

If you are using powdered wheat paste, be sure to mix it about 30 minutes to an hour before using; the paste will adhere better if its ingredients are thoroughly integrated. Slowly add powder to a bucket or pail of cold water. In most cases, you should mix paste a bit thicker than manufacturer's specifications. Reducing the amount of water will make for better adhesion, and provide a slicker, easier-to-manipulate surface to move the paper into position. Stir with your hand until the paste has an even, creamy consistency and is free of lumps.

Because they must guarantee their jobs, most professional paperhangers and decorating contractors use paste even with prepasted paper; if you want to be absolutely certain of the permanence of your work, you may wish to do the same. For best results, use a premixed vinyl adhesive and thin with water in a ratio of about 1 part water to 2 parts paste, depending on the stiffness of the paper (make the paste thicker for stiffer paper). The paste that's already on the paper will supply added sticking power.

Generally, a pound of dry mix will provide enough paste for about 6 rolls of wallpaper; a gallon of vinyl adhesive will cover from 2 to 3 rolls less, depending on the weight and porosity of the backing.

TECHNIQUES: PASTING

Pasting Paper

Work with one strip at a time. Place it pattern down on your table and clamp the top. Using a thick-nap roller, apply paste to the strip. Even application is extremely important to make certain the paper adheres uniformly to the wall. Securing the paper with your free hand, roll the paste toward the edges and clamped end of the strip. Use a damp sponge to wipe up excess paste. When you've finished the top half of the strip, fold it back against itself so the end is at the middle of the strip. Turn the strip around, clamp the unpasted end, and paste the other half.

Booking and Curing Paper

When you've finished pasting the strip, unclamp and lightly fold the second half so the ends of the strip meet—but do not overlap—roughly in the middle. Align the edges but do not crease the folds. This folding process, called "booking," helps spread paste evenly and reduce water evaporation while the paper "cures." The booked paper should sit for about 10 minutes. Besides softening the paper for easier handling, curing allows each strip to expand to its fullest dimensions. This is especially important with prepasted papers, which otherwise can swell ¼ inch or more on your walls. Note: if selvage must be trimmed, lightly place a steel straightedge along the trim marks and slit through both layers of the booked paper with a razor knife (use a fresh blade each time).

Using a Water Box

If you decide against pasting prepasted paper (see opposite page), you can use a plastic or metal dip trough (available from your dealer) to moisten the dry paste. Half-fill the trough with lukewarm water and place it on the floor directly in front of the area to be covered. Beginning at bottom edge, roll up a cut wallpaper strip, pattern side in, and immerse in water. Soak according to paper manufacturer's specifications. Pull paper out top first.

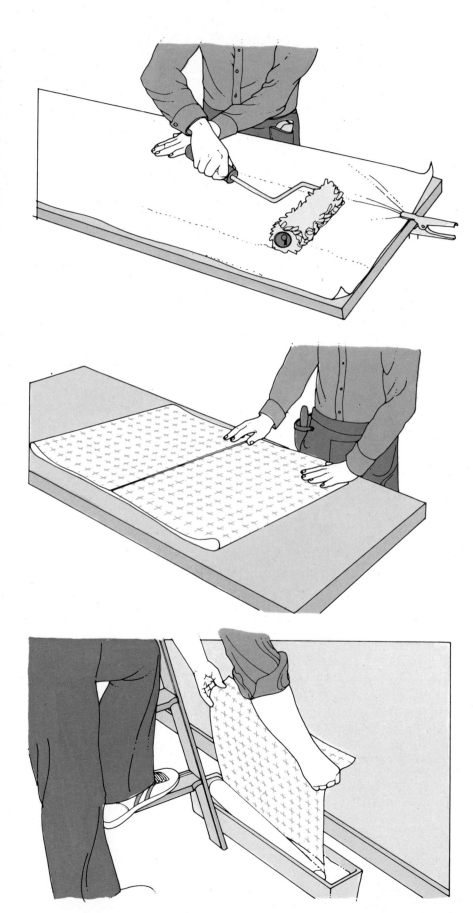

TECHNIQUES: THE FIRST STRIP

Hanging the First Strip

1. Standing on stepladder, unfold the top section of your booked paper and gently push the paper against the top of the wall, following the professional's "rule of four"—always have 2 inches of excess at both top and bottom. Tack the strip in place—that is, wipe it lightly with a dampened sponge or brush, but do not smooth it flat. With flocked or embossed papers, pat lightly with a folded cloth to avoid surface damage. See if the strip's edge lines up with the plumb line. Don't worry if the strip isn't straight; wallpaper paste dries slowly. Lift and shift the paper until it is aligned.

2. Using your smoothing brush, stroke the paper flat against the top of the wall. Then smooth the paper with downward strokes, working from the center out toward the sides. Gently lift the bottom of the strip away from the wall to free the paper of wrinkles created by the brushing.

Top of strip

Smoothing brush

3. Release the bottom fold, sliding the paper into position with the palms of your hands. Recheck the alignment and adjust if necessary. Press the remainder of the strip against the wall with the smoothing brush, again working out from the center.

4. Working from the center to the edges, smooth the entire strip with a damp sponge to remove flecks of paste and air bubbles. Wait to trim the paper until you have hung the second strip.

Bottom of strip

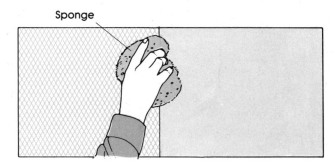

Sponge

Close-up on Trimming

To trim the hung strips, use a wide drywall knife as a guide and cut with a razor knife, changing blades frequently. Hold the razor knife in your right hand (reverse if you're left-handed), and the broad knife in your left. Pressing the broad knife as flat against the wall as possible, pull the razor knife along the straight edge provided by the broad knife. Then, without lifting the razor knife from its cutting groove, "leapfrog" the broad knife to the front of the cutting line. Continue leapfrogging the broad knife and cutting with the razor knife until the trim is complete. *Remember to change blades with every cut.* Expect to use 30 or 40 razor blades per room. It's a lot cheaper and less frustrating than tearing paper.

Razor knife

Door or window frame

TECHNIQUES: THE SECOND STRIP

Three Kinds of Seams

Butt seam. The butt seam is the usual way of joining wallpaper. Slide the new strip tightly against the previously hung paper until the edges form a slight ridge but do not overlap. Don't stretch the paper. Wait 15 or 20 minutes, then flatten with a seam roller.

Lap seam. The lap joint is rarely used today except in inside corners that are not truly vertical, where a butt seam would leave a gap. A variation of the lap joint, called the "wire edge," overlaps adjacent strips by 1/8 or 1/16 inch. The wire edge can be useful if your paper shrinks a great deal. To determine if shrinkage is a problem, wait about 30 minutes after hanging the second strip. If a gap appears between it and the first strip, use the wire edge seam.

Double-cut seam. Professionals sometimes use a seaming technique called double cutting that produces a perfect fit (but a pattern mismatch is almost inevitable). Double cutting must be used in place of a lapped seam with all-vinyl paper; vinyl coverings will not adhere to themselves. Lap the second strip about ½ inch over the first strip. Then, using a straightedge and with a fresh blade in your razor knife, cut down the middle of the lapped paper. Pull off the top piece. Run the razor back down the cutting line. Lift the outer paper and peel out the narrow underlying piece. Smooth both strips back into place and flatten with a seam roller. Never double-cut over previously papered walls.

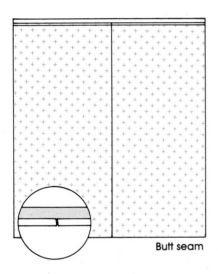

Butt seam

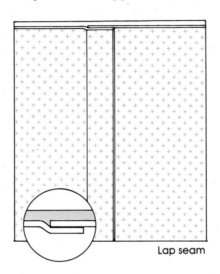

Lap seam

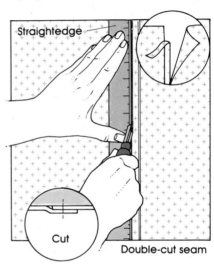

Straightedge

Cut

Double-cut seam

Hanging the Second Strip

1. Tack the paper into position at the ceiling, then slide it (use the palms of your hands in the center of the strip, rather than at the edges) against the first strip until the edges fit as snugly as possible without overlapping (if you're using butt seams), or lap the strips (if you're using lapped or double-cut seams).

2. Smooth the paper and trim the excess off both first and second strips at baseboards and ceiling, using a broad knife and razor knife as described at left. Flatten the edges with a seam roller (or a cloth or sponge if working with flocked or raised papers). Press lightly to avoid a glossy streak. Sponge away excess paste and air bubbles (use a smoothing brush on flocked or embossed papers).

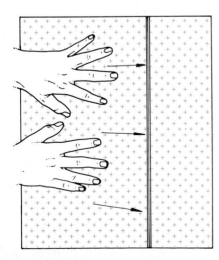

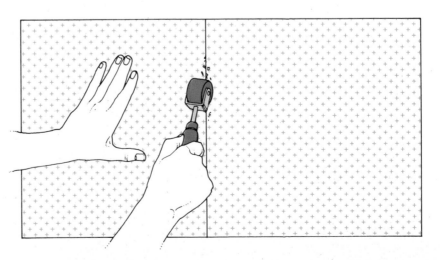

Because they present few obstacles other than a central light fixture, ceilings are an easy job for professional paperhangers. But working overhead can be difficult for someone less familiar with papering; in most cases, the cheaper and easier alternative of painting should be carefully considered. If the case for a papered ceiling seems compelling, you'll find small, nondirectional patterns easiest to work with. Be sure you have an energetic helper. To avoid spoiling your other work, always paper the ceiling *before* papering or painting walls.

Planning placement. Hang your paper across the ceiling's narrowest dimension—that way you'll be working with the shortest strips possible. The first strip will lap down onto the narrow wall 1 inch. Allowing for that inch, measure the width of the first strip and lightly mark the ceiling at each end, 1¼ inches from the long walls. Push tacks into the marks and stretch chalked string between them. Pull the string down and snap it against the ceiling to make a straight guideline. Cut all the strips to the same length, following the "rule of four" by adding 2 inches top and bottom for trimmable excess.

Hanging the paper. Erect a scaffold using a plank and two stepladders, or a stepladder and a sawhorse. Apply paste to the first strip and book it or fold it accordion-style. Line the strip up with the guideline and put it in place—allowing the 2-inch overlap at each end and 1 inch along the width—with your helper supporting the paper from behind. Brush flat into corners. Gently loosen paper in corners and make a "box" cut in each about 1 inch by 2 inches. Smooth the paper. If you will be papering the walls, trim the excess to ½ inch; if not, trim to the ceiling. Paste and hang remaining strips.

Plumb lines

Snapping a plumb line

TECHNIQUES: CORNERS

Because corners are rarely plumb, you'll need to take special care when papering around them. In most cases, it's a bad idea to "wrap" a full width of wallpaper around a corner; you're likely to wind up with wrinkled paper or a severely mismatched pattern, often both. A better approach is to divide corner widths lengthwise into sections A and B, hanging them separately, as shown in the illustrations below.

Cutting Sections A and B

At both the top and bottom of the wall, measure the distance between the edge of the nearest strip hung and the corner. For inside corners, add ½ inch to the widest dimension; for outside corners, add 1 inch (unless your paper is particularly stiff, as some vinyls and foils are, in which case an outside corner requires a 4-inch to 6-inch overlap). Using your straightedge, cut a strip of wallpaper lengthwise into a section A width equal to this figure; the remainder is section B. If the remainder is less than 6 inches wide, however, use a full-width strip for your section B.

Hanging Section A

Inside corner. Apply paste and press section A into the corner, smoothing the ½-inch excess width around to the other wall.

Outside corner. Smooth section A into place and, with a fresh razor blade, cut top and bottom slits exactly at the ceiling and baseboard corners. Fold the strip around the corner and trim the top and bottom excess.

Restriking Plumb

To restore vertical alignment, measure the width of section B and add ¼ inch. Measure that distance from the corner along the new wall and snap a plumb line using chalked string. (The extra ¼ inch assures that the chalk line will not coincide with the seam.)

Hanging Section B

Using the plumb line as a guide and overlapping section A where it extends beyond the corner, hang section B. There will probably be a slight mismatch where the sections meet, unless the corner is perfectly vertical. Use the lapped seam technique unless you are hanging vinyl wallpaper, in which case double-cut the seam (see page 75).

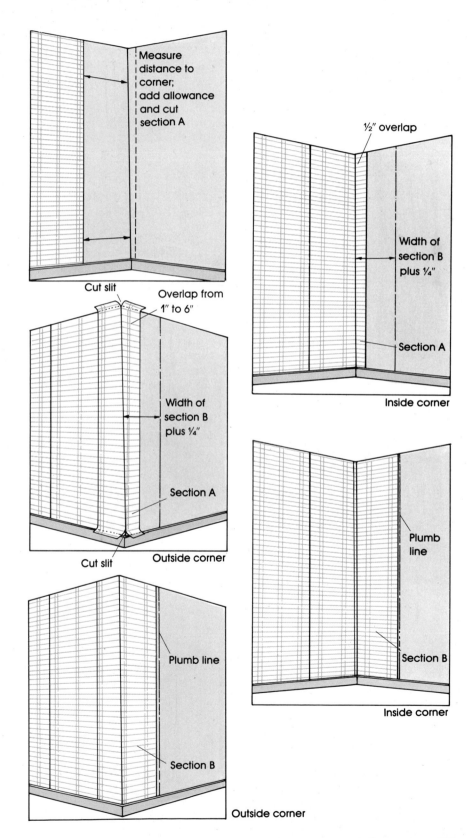

Measure distance to corner; add allowance and cut section A

Cut slit

Overlap from 1″ to 6″

Width of section B plus ¼″

Section A

Cut slit

Outside corner

Plumb line

Section B

Outside corner

½″ overlap

Width of section B plus ¼″

Section A

Inside corner

Plumb line

Section B

Inside corner

TECHNIQUES: WINDOWS

No room is made up solely of flat surfaces. Sooner or later you'll run into a series of obstacles, such as windows, doors, cabinets or bookshelves, arches, slanted walls, stairwells, lighting fixtures, and rafters. Instructions for coping with these room elements appear on the next six pages.

Papering around windows with moldings (or doors, cabinets, or built-in bookshelves) is a fairly straightforward process. However, when windows are recessed and thus have no moldings, as is common in modern homes, the technique is more complicated. For that reason, papering jobs in rooms with recessed windows require careful preplanning. The technique described in this section will work with deep and shallow recessed windows and with vinyl or standard wallpapers (but with vinyl coverings you must use vinyl-to-vinyl paste, available from your dealer).

With either kind of window (but especially with recessed ones) you can make your job easier by avoiding complicated patterns with long vertical repeats. Don't try to precut the paper to go around the window; with any obstacle, paper is easiest to cut when it is up. Metal window frames should not be papered; wooden sills should be painted or given a natural wood finish.

If you find you have difficulty papering around obstacles, don't panic. Stay calm, step back, and rethink what you're doing. Remember that, until it has dried, wallpaper can almost always be shifted.

Windows With Moldings

1. Align a new, pasted strip against the last strip hung, positioning it at the ceiling and loosely pressing it into place around the window. Using a razor blade, cut away the paper along the lines of the opening, allowing a 2-inch excess for trimming. Using a fresh razor blade, cut 45-degree diagonal slits at the top and bottom of the cut edge to the outer corners of the molding, ending exactly at the molding's edge.

2. Press the paper against the side of the molding with the bristles of a smoothing brush, then trim away the excess with a wide drywall knife and razor knife. Trim the paper as close as possible to the frame, but leave a hairline gap between the frame and the paper.

3. Shape the paper around the rounded edge of the bottom sill by making small cuts in the paper and pressing it tightly against the molding with your fingers. Trim it flush to the molding. Paper the areas above and below the window with short strips. Adjust the strips on the wall to achieve an exact pattern match and trim the excess from the tops and bottoms. Smooth and sponge off excess paste. When the remaining unpapered space is less than the full width of a strip, paper the opposite side of the window as described above.

Note: use the technique described above to paper around such elements as doors, cabinets, and built-in bookshelves.

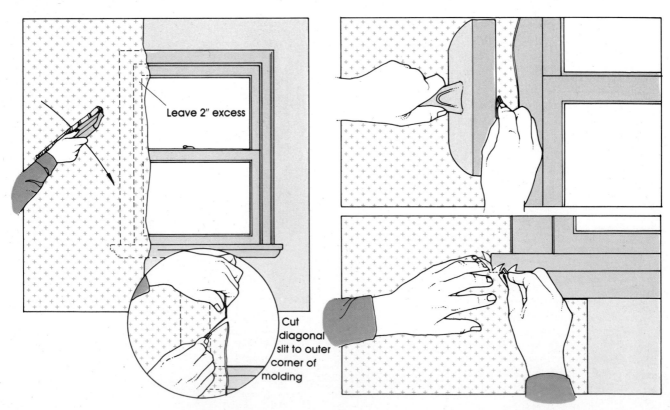

Leave 2″ excess

Cut diagonal slit to outer corner of molding

Recessed Windows

1. Using your tape measure and pencil, plan your job with the first strip of paper on the left inside (recessed) edge of the window, allowing 2 inches of overlap for trimming. Working away from the window, mark off full wallpaper widths for succeeding strips, letting the less-than-full-width strip fall at the nearest corner of the room. Strike a plumb line for the first strip. Cut two triangles to fit the corners of the recess and paste them up as shown. Remember, if you are using vinyl paper, you must use vinyl-to-vinyl paste.

2. Hang the first strip, smoothing it onto the wall next to, above, and below the window. Make certain you've allowed enough paper to reach the recessed window casing, plus 2 inches. Using your fingers, feel through the paper and locate the upper outside corner of the window. With a fresh razor blade, cut a 45-degree slit from the corner to the edge of the paper. Do the same at the window's bottom corner. With your fingers, tuck and smooth the paper into the recess; make certain paper is pressed firmly against casing.

3. Hang paper across the top and bottom of the window as if you were putting up full-length strips. Note: with drop-match patterns, you'll need to alternate strips (skip ahead one strip on the roll) to achieve a perfect match.

4. Cut the paper away from the center area of the window (save the scrap, it may come in handy for repairs), leaving 2 inches of excess at the top and bottom. Smooth the paper into the recess and against the casing. Cut triangles and paste them into the upper and lower corners of the opposite side of the window as described in Step 1. Finish papering the opposite side of the window as described in Step 2. Using your razor knife (with a fresh blade), trim away excess paper all around the window, cutting as closely as possible to the casing to avoid gaps. Wipe away excess paste with a damp sponge.

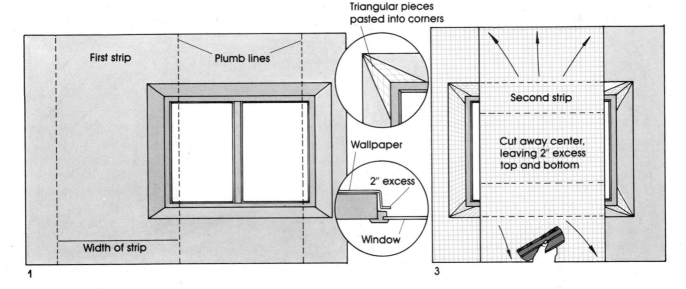

First strip | Plumb lines | Triangular pieces pasted into corners | Wallpaper | 2" excess | Window | Width of strip

Second strip | Cut away center, leaving 2" excess top and bottom

1 · 3

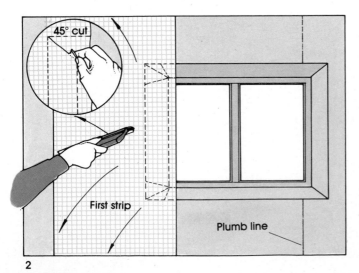

45° cut · First strip · Plumb line

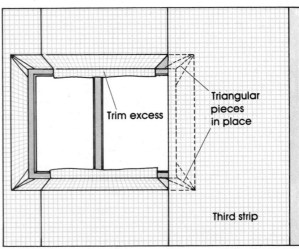

Trim excess · Triangular pieces in place · Third strip

2 · 4

TECHNIQUES: ARCHES & SLANTED WALLS

Redoing an entire home may well mean working with irregular shapes such as arches, slanted ceilings, and stairwells, in which case the easiest procedure is prob-ably to paint. If, nonetheless, you choose to paper, you'll need to learn some new techniques in addition to match-ing, pasting, and seaming.

Arches

1. Paper the area above and around the arch as you would any wall, allowing the strips to hang into the archway opening. When the full width of the arch has been covered, trim the excess paper so it overlaps the edge by 2 inches.

2. Snip small triangular "teeth" out of the overlap, cutting from the edge of the paper to the edge of the arch, and spacing the teeth more closely where the curve is the sharpest. Turn the teeth under, smoothing them firmly into place against the inside of the arch.

Using a razor knife (with a fresh blade), trim the teeth to an overall length of ½ inch.

3. Cut a strip of paper slightly nar-rower than the width of the arch (to avoid peeling). Paste into place, covering all the teeth.

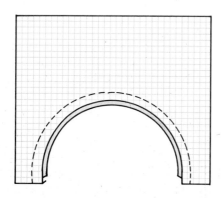

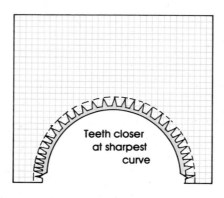

Teeth closer at sharpest curve

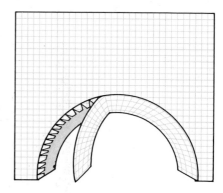

Slanted Walls

You'll find a small-scale or nondirectional pattern easiest to hang on slanted walls; buy an extra roll for good measure. Finish papering the wall adjacent to the slanted area, leaving a ½-inch overlap on the slanted wall. Add ¼ inch to the width of a wallpaper roll, mea-sure this distance from the inside corner, and snap plumb lines on the slanted and knee walls. Cut and paste strips for the slanted part of the wall first, overlapping ¼ inch down onto the knee wall, then put up the knee wall strips.

Turn the outside corner as described on page 77, doing the slanted part of the wall first, then the knee wall. You'll have to cut ceiling and baseboard slits so that the paper can wrap slightly (about 1 inch) without wrinkling. Fill in the triangular area formed on the adjacent wall by the slant, using full widths of paper if possible. Using a fresh razor, trim diagonally along the slant—slicing "freehand" is the best approach—and horizontally at the ceiling.

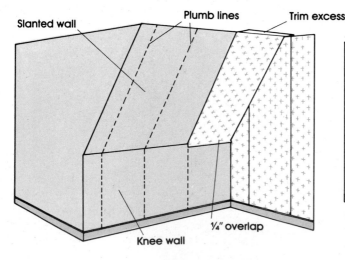

Slanted wall

Plumb lines

Trim excess

Knee wall

¼" overlap

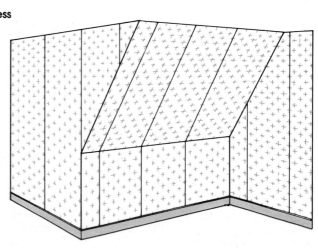

Plan on finding a helper if you decide to paper a stairwell. Hanging 12-foot- and 14-foot-long, paste-heavy strips of wallpaper can be an arm-wearying job for a person working alone. You'll also need to rig a scaffold (see below). Otherwise the job is the same as papering any other wall.

Stairwells

Measure, match, and cut all strips before hanging. For well wall strips, measure longest vertical distance to diagonal baseboard for each strip, plus 2 inches top and bottom. Drop a plumb line at the beginning of the well wall. Paste and book all well and head wall strips and, using the scaffold, work from the first well wall strip toward the corner of the head wall.

Hang and trim the tops of the strips first, working from the scaffold. Have your helper unfold and smooth into place the bottoms of the strips. Paper the inner corner in the same manner as described on page 77, but to help in handling its greater-than-normal length, cut your section A as you would trim selvage, with the paper pasted and booked (see page 73). Hang the top of section A, cutting a 1-inch slit at the top to allow the overlap to wrap onto the head wall. Use the remainder of the strip as section B. (Do not use a full width of wallpaper as section B or you're almost certain to end up with a partial strip at the outside head wall corner, a prominent focal point.)

Roll the seams and trim the well wall paper at the baseboard. Trim the head wall strips flush at the bottom of the wall, leaving no excess to turn under. Note: if you are working with flocked or embossed patterns, using a seam roller can damage the edges; press such coverings down with a damp sponge or moistened cloth.

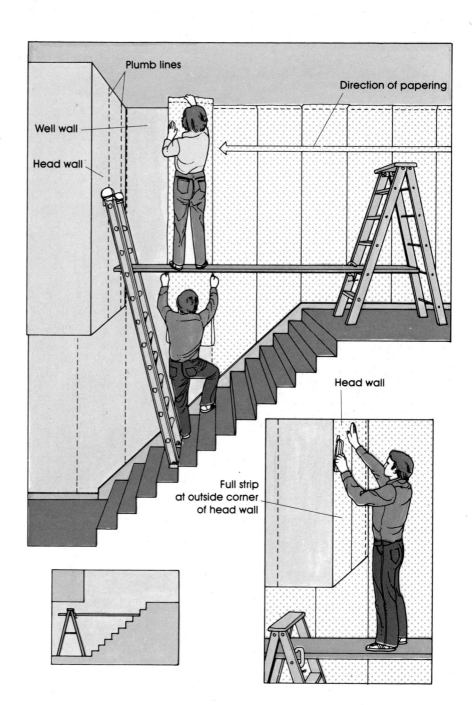

Plumb lines

Direction of papering

Well wall

Head wall

Head wall

Full strip at outside corner of head wall

How to Rig Your Own Scaffold

Two ordinary 5-foot stepladders, a stepladder and a sawhorse, or a straight ladder and a staircase—any of these combinations can be used with a 12-inch by 10-foot plank (with no knotholes) to erect a temporary scaffold. If you're using a stepladder, remember to make sure the spreader bars are locked in place and, if you're working near a door, make sure it's fully open to avoid any unwanted surprises. Follow the other safety pointers on page 29.

TECHNIQUES: OBSTACLES

The quality of your papering around obstacles will go a long way toward determining the effect of your job. Never try to precut paper to fit around obstacles; papering *under* light fixtures and electrical installations will yield the most professional results. In general, that will require removal of switch and outlet covers and loosening of fixture baseplates. Be sure to turn off the power when disconnecting fixtures, and be cautious when working with sponges, watery pastes, and metallic wall coverings around switches and outlets.

Electrical Switches and Outlets

1. After removing switches and outlet covers, prime them with a vinyl-to-vinyl latex primer—a special wall-preparation material for pasting vinyl wallcoverings to plastic or similar slick surfaces. Wait one hour until the primer dries.

2. Paper the wall as you would normally, covering right over the switch or outlet box. Cut an *X* across the face of the box, stopping about ¼ inch in from the corners. Trim the flaps of the *X* away, forming a hole about ¼ inch smaller than the opening.

3. Experiment with some paper scraps and the plate against the wall until you find a piece that can be cut to match the pattern surrounding the switch box. Cut it slightly larger than the plate, fold it lightly over the top of the plate, and match the top edge to its adjacent pattern on the wall. Unfold the paper and slide it down on the plate ⅛ inch; fold it firmly over both top and bottom. This ⅛-inch adjustment allows for a near match at both top and bottom; if you have an exact match on one edge, the curve of the plate produces an obvious mismatch on the opposite edge. Follow the same procedure in matching the sides, folding one side, then shifting the paper ⅛ inch and refolding.

4. Place the paper face down and paste. Center the cover plate inside the folded lines. Cut away the corners and fold the edges over the back of the plate, pressing firmly.

5. When the plate is dry, cut *X*'s for the switch and outlet openings, pasting the untrimmed flaps onto the back of the plate. Use a pin to punch through the screw holes; remount the plate to the wall.

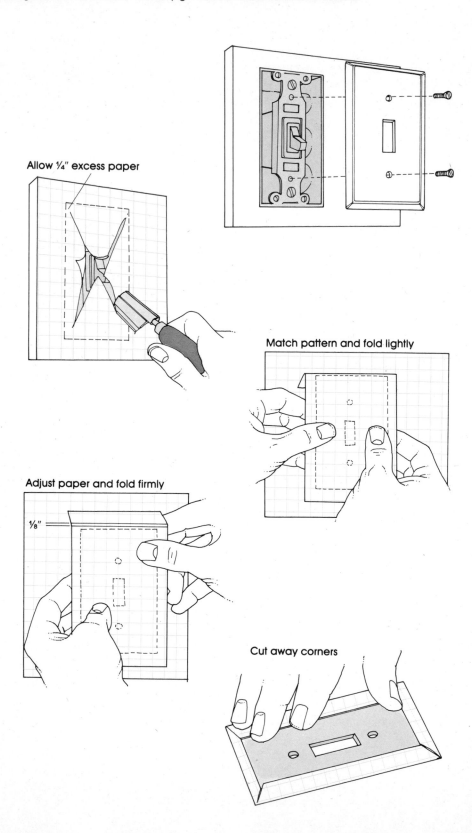

Allow ¼" excess paper

Match pattern and fold lightly

Adjust paper and fold firmly

⅛"

Cut away corners

Light Fixtures

1. Shut the power off. Remove the fixture cover, light bulbs, and baseplate screws. Remove the screws that mount the fixture to the electrical box. Unscrew the small plastic caps connecting fixture wires by turning counterclockwise. (In older homes, wires may simply be twisted together.

Disconnect the wires, using rubber gloves and insulated pliers. When you are ready to reconnect the wires, install small plastic caps.) Do not disturb the unshielded ground wire attached to the electrical box. Carefully take the fixture down from the ceiling, keeping the parts together as much as possible.

2. Paper over the area as you would normally, smoothing the paper over the electrical box and then cutting an *X* as described at left. Finish by trimming the opening around the inside edges of the box.

3. Reinstall the fixture (see illustration), reconnecting the wires.

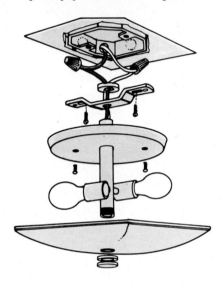

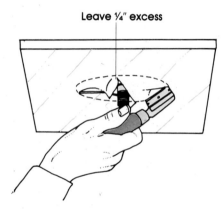

Leave ¼" excess

Bring ends together; turn cap clockwise

Exposed Beams or Rafters

1. Position the paper at the ceiling with the normal 2-inch excess and smooth it against the side of the rafter, lightly folding it at the break between the rafter and the wall. To fit the paper around the rafter, make a slit in the paper, cutting outward from the lowest edge of the rafter to the top edge of the paper at a slight diagonal. Smooth the paper into

place against the upper wall, but do not open the strip if it is booked. Using a razor knife and broad knife, slit the paper underneath and then alongside the rafter where it meets the wall. End the slit exactly at the farthest bottom edge of the rafter.

2. Loosen the paper from alongside the rafter and swing it underneath and around the

rafter's other side. Smooth the paper into place, working snugly against the wall and rafter and trimming with a razor knife as needed. If the strip was booked, unbook the lower part now. Smooth the remainder of the paper into place. Trim the excess paper at the ceiling and sponge off excess paste. The sides of the rafter are especially likely to be smeared.

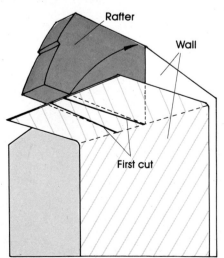

Rafter

Wall

First cut

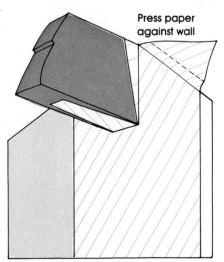

Press paper against wall

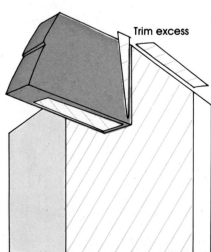

Trim excess

When you've finished hanging your last strip, step back and give your work a careful inspection. No matter how good a job you've done, there are bound to be some small flaws. The most common problems with freshly hung paper are air blisters, loose edges, and small tears.

If you've made a large tear while hanging the paper, you should replace the entire strip. But once the paste has dried, large tears can be repaired by the process described below. Remember, too, to save those wallpaper scraps; they may come in handy for future repairs.

Blisters and Bubbles

Air bubbles and blisters are isolated flaws and should be distinguished from *wrinkles*, which result from the paper's shifting. Wrinkles are often caused by uneven absorption of moisture from the paste, a possible indication that the underlying wall surface may have been sealed inadequately. A wrinkled strip must be removed and repositioned while the adhesive is still wet. *Never attempt to eliminate a wrinkle by stretching or pulling at the paper.* Chances are, when the paste dries, the paper will resume its original position, leaving you to cope with gaps between seams and the original wrinkle as well.

Air blisters and bubbles should be eliminated in the hanging process; push the air out of one strip with your broad knife before hanging the next strip. However, if the dried paste has trapped air that can't be smoothed out, use a fresh razor blade to make a slit. Try to cut at an angle, and choose a part of the pattern where the slit will be least noticeable. Use an artist's brush to apply white glue to both the wall surface and the underside of the paper and use a seam roller to press the wallpaper into place. Wipe the area with a damp sponge.

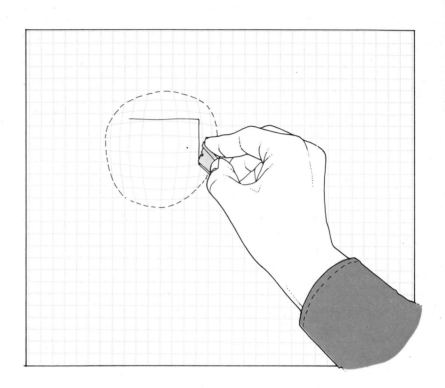

Loose Edges and Small Tears

Small tears and loose edges are easy to fix. Just apply white glue or paste to the underside of the paper and to the wall surface and press the paper into place with a seam roller. Be careful not to crease the paper. Wipe away excess adhesive with a damp sponge.

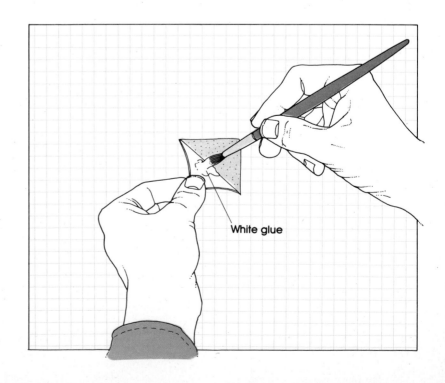

White glue

Large Tears and Damaged Areas

1. Adjust a larger piece of wallpaper over the damaged area until the patterns match; tack into place with masking tape.

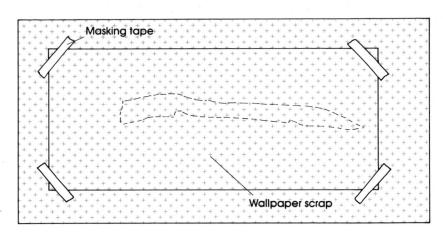

Masking tape

Wallpaper scrap

2. Using a metal straightedge, cut through both layers with a fresh razor blade. Remove the masking tape and patch. Lift out the damaged section of wallpaper and clean the underlying wall area. Use a putty knife to scrape any remaining wallpaper from the patch area.

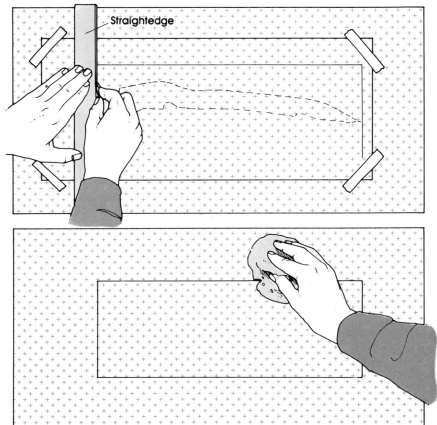

Straightedge

3. Apply paste or glue to the patch and carefully position it against the wall. The pattern should match. Using your fingers or a seam roller, smooth the patch firmly into place. Remove excess glue with a damp sponge.

Maintaining Wallpaper

Every six months to a year, wallpaper should be cleaned according to the manufacturer's instructions. You can use mild soap and water, commercial cleaners, cleaning dough, or spot removers, all available from your local dealer. Whichever cleaner you choose, try a little in an area of the wallpaper that doesn't show—behind a large chair or sofa, perhaps—to make sure the cleaner doesn't damage your paper's color or texture. When removing stains from nonwashable paper, blot the soiled area with a sponge dipped in mild soap and cold water, blot again with a clear water rinse, and pat the area dry with a clean cloth.

You can apply a clear protective coating, available from your dealer, that makes it possible to scrub non-washable paper. Such coatings can help safeguard patched and high-wear areas, but to avoid problems with mildew, do not apply any coating until underlying paste has dried, usually about a week.

SPECIAL EFFECTS: MURALS

Mural wallpapers have a single, large design printed across a number of strips; they are often big enough to cover an entire wall. Nature scenes and *trompe l'oeil* (French for "fool the eye," pronounced *tromPLAY*) effects are among the most popular forms of murals. Especially effective in opening up small rooms, murals are usually far less costly than mirrors, an alternative space expander. Murals can also dress up large, unbroken walls—in a family room, perhaps—or establish a more formal tone—in an office lobby, for example. Available in color and in black and white, murals are usually sold boxed as separate strips rather than as rolls. They come in a variety of materials—cloth-backed vinyl, paper, and foil, to name a few. Most murals include throwaway panels (strips that can be eliminated without sacrificing the design) so they can be hung on walls of varying lengths.

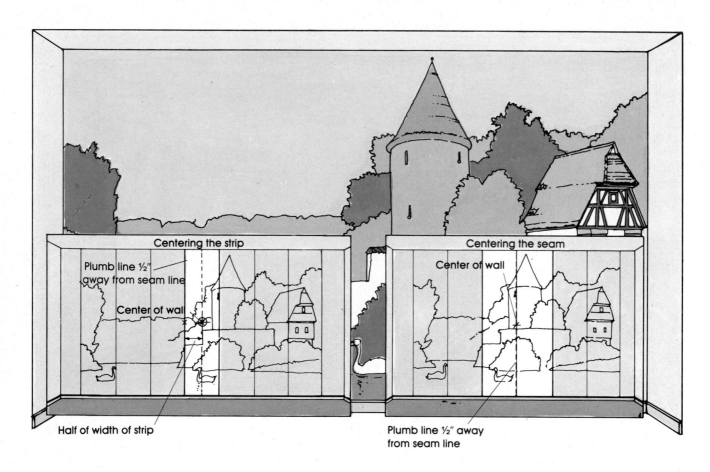

Centering the strip
Plumb line ½" away from seam line
Center of wall
Half of width of strip

Centering the seam
Center of wall
Plumb line ½" away from seam line

Hanging Murals

Before hanging a mural you must prepare a smooth wall surface; underlying unevenness can destroy the pictorial effect. Sand or fill in walls with joint compound to remove any roughness, then apply lining paper (see page 66) according to the manufacturer's instructions. Try to get someone to help you when you start hanging the mural.

First, figure out how many panels will fit on your wall and put them in manufacturer's recommended sequence. To find the most pleasing vertical placement for the mural, you'll have to proceed by trial and error. Hold the strip with the design's highest point against the wall and move it up and down until you find the best placement. Make light pencil marks on the paper at the ceiling break and baseboard. Hold the next panel adjacent to the marked strip. When the designs match exactly, mark the second strip as you did the first. Continue until ceiling and baseboard cutoff points are marked on every strip. Add 4 inches for top and bottom excess and cut all the panels accordingly.

In most cases, you should position a mural so that the design is centered on the wall. To accomplish this, measure off and lightly mark an *X* at the center of the wall. If the length of your wall calls for an even number of strips, the center line should fall exactly on the line where the two middle strips meet. Carefully snap a plumb line ½ inch away from the *X*. (Precise vertical alignment is crucial to hanging any mural.) If the number of strips needed to cover the wall is odd, the center line should bisect the middle panel. Measure half a strip's width to the left of the *X*. Snap a plumb line ½ inch from this point. Hang the mural as you would any butt-seamed wallpaper.

SPECIAL EFFECTS: BORDERS

Besides murals, of course, wallpaper offers a world of other ways of making something look like what it's not. Some papers can be used to finish the lower part of the wall in a dado that looks like old-fashioned paneling. Others can be used to create a border-molding effect at the ceiling line or around otherwise plain closet doors. Ceiling borders are usually pasted and booked in full lengths and then hung starting from an inconspicuous corner as described on page 68.

Borders

Borders can be used in conjunction with a compatible wallcovering or by themselves. Either way, a border usually defines an area—around a window or central entryway, for example—or accents the break between different materials—a wallpapered upper wall, say, with wainscoting below. By far the most common place for borders, however, is around the tops of walls at the ceiling break. Borders tend to confine space, so they may not be the best design choice for a small room.

Borders are sold separately, from special narrow rolls, or as part of a wallpaper design printed on the same roll. Either way, borders must be trimmed. Very complicated patterns may require a knife, but for the great majority of borders, the same scissors you use for regular wallpaper will do. Trimming a border can be time-consuming and tedious; don't plan to trim and hang a border on the same day. Trim first, then set the border aside until you're fresh.

Hanging a ceiling border. You'll need a helper to hang a ceiling border. First, paste the entire back of the border and then fold it like an accordion, being careful not to crease the edges. While your assistant holds the folded border, begin hanging it at a corner behind or beside a door. Press the paper into place with your hands and continue around the room, creasing the border into the corners as you go. Go back and make any minor shifts and adjustments, and then smooth the border firmly into place with a damp sponge, wiping away excess paste.

A wallpaper border featuring children's-book covers lines the ceiling break of this child's bedroom, with matching fabric at the window.

FABRIC PANELS

Fabric wallcoverings can be time-consuming to install, but they generally last longer than paper and can be less expensive as well. Padded with cotton or polyester batting, fabric can reduce both noise levels and energy bills. Moreover, fabric can add richness to an otherwise austere room. Virtually any type of cloth will work. In general, stapling and shirring on rods are the easiest methods of application for a beginner; pasting, which is sometimes required for expensive cloth wallcoverings, is probably best left to professionals. You'll find nondirectional patterns simplest to work with because you won't have to worry about repeats. To keep your cutting instruments sharp, always use separate scissors for padding and fabric. Keep your tools clean and use a soft brush to smooth the material. Most of today's fabrics can be used as they come from the bolt without separate washing or sizing, but they should be ironed just before hanging. Use a hand-steamer for on-the-wall touchups later.

Padded Fabric Panels

Stapling fabric to individual panels provides firm, stable support for the material and facilitates the repair of stained or damaged wallcoverings; you simply replace the flawed panel. For lightweight, maneuverable panels, use ½-inch-thick soundboard, available at most lumber yards in 4 by 8 sheets, and ¼-inch-thick foam sheeting for padding. Plan to center focal point panels over the fireplace or between windows and end in an inconspicuous spot such as near a door (see page 69 on centering).

Save the final panel until all the others are up, then cut it to fit the exact space; wall dimensions do vary, particularly in older homes, and your padded panels may not come out exactly the width you planned on. Paneling is basically a technique for fairly simple walls with few obstacles to work around; you would be well advised not to use it in a room with irregular walls or special features such as arches.

1. Determine the desired dimensions of each panel (they'll vary, of course, but try to work with panels not much more than an arm's length wide—40 inches, say—and 5 or 6 feet tall). Use a hand or power saw to cut the soundboard as precisely as possible. To allow for light fixtures and other protruding objects, gouge a hole in the soundboard with a screwdriver or utility knife, then finish cutting out with a keyhole saw. For a more elegant look, bevel the edges of the soundboard with a sanding block or rasp. With a pair of scissors (not the same ones used to cut fabric), trim a piece of foam sheeting 2 inches larger than the panel being covered. Starting with the longest sides and working from the center, staple the foam to the soundboard. Pull the foam toward corners and wrap tightly around the panel. Snip a triangle from the "dog ears" by making one cut parallel to the panel and a second cut at a right angle to the first. Flatten down the remaining fabric and staple firmly.

2. Cut the fabric in sections 2 inches larger than each panel, iron and place face down on a clean surface. Lay the panel, foam down, on top of the fabric. Staple the left vertical side of the panel, working from the center toward the corners. "Dog ears" should stand up at the corners; if they don't, the fabric isn't tight enough, and you should pull it out and restaple. Cut a triangle out of the dog ears as with the foam, then staple flat.

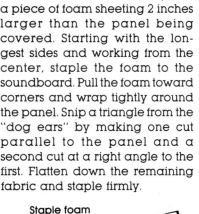

Staple foam to soundboard

Staple out from center

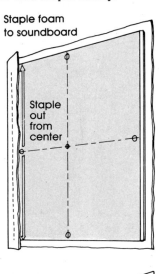

Staple fabric over foam

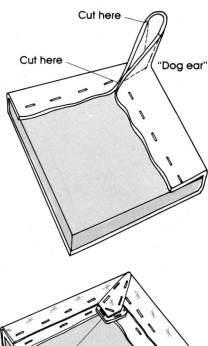

Cut here

Cut here

"Dog ear"

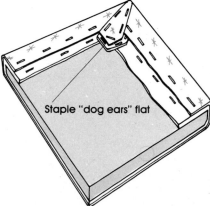

Staple "dog ears" flat

3. To mount panels permanently, attach at least three horizontal rows of ¼-inch-thick furring strips to the wall. Nail the furring into studs or use expansion bolts. Position the strips so that they divide the panel area into thirds. If you don't wish to mount the panels permanently, attach the furring with heavy double-sided tape—it may fail in particularly high or low temperatures, though—or silicone caulking adhesive. Don't use glues or strong adhesives;

they will damage plaster or wallboard should furring strips be removed.

4. Temporarily work panels into place, pushing from left to right and back again. Panels should fit snugly enough to stay in place but not so tightly that they bulge. Uneven spots in underlying soundboard can cause poor fit; flatten such areas with a hammer and a flat piece of wood, or pry the fabric and foam away from the panel and shave the soundboard with a utility knife.

5. When you're satisfied with the fit, mount the panels to the furring strips using parquet floor adhesive. Be careful to work in a well-ventilated area; this extra-heavy cement is nonflammable, but it gives off powerful fumes. Apply the adhesive with a putty knife; three thick dollops across each furring strip should do. To ensure a strong bond, temporarily fasten the panels to the furring strips with ¾-inch upholstery tacks. Put small squares of construction paper or filing cards between the tacks and the fabric to help you remove the tacks after the adhesive has dried overnight.

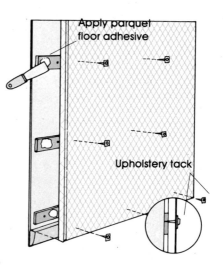

Apply parquet floor adhesive

Upholstery tack

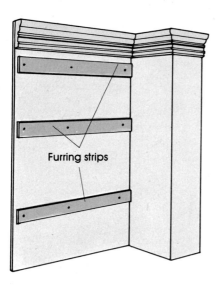

Furring strips

How to Figure Yardage

Here's a step-by-step way to calculate how much yardage you'll need. Think in terms of strips whether you plan to use padded panels or staple your fabric directly to the walls.

1. Add the total length of all walls to measure the perimeter of the room *in inches*.

2. Divide by the width of the fabric *in inches* to determine how many individual fabric strips you'll need to go around the room. (Note: if you are using padded panels, before doing the division, subtract about 4 inches from the fabric width to allow for wrapping around the board.)

3. Multiply by the height of the wall (plus 4 inches to allow for top and bottom excess) to determine the total inches of fabric you'll need to purchase.

4. Divide by 36 inches to convert the total fabric requirement into yards. Round out to the next full yard and, for safety's sake, add enough extra material for at least one additional strip.

Pattern repeats. When figuring yardage, you'll need to allow extra material for pattern repeats. Round to the closest even number of times the pattern will cover the height of each vertical section you're covering. As with wallpaper, in most cases, the larger the repeat, the more material you'll have to waste. To calculate the repeat, divide the inches between the repeats into the height of the wall area you're covering. Include the 4 inches allowed for excess. Thus, assuming the wall area is 80 inches high and the repeat is 32 inches:

$$80 + 4 = 84 \div 32 = 2.53$$

Three repeats per panel of fabric are required, with 12 inches of wasted material per section ($3 \times 32 = 96 - 84 = 12$). Obviously, if economy were your sole criterion, you would try to choose a fabric with a pattern repeat exactly matching your dimensions, but that's very difficult. An easier solution is to choose a solid color or a pattern with vertical stripes, so that pattern repeat is not a consideration.

BACKTACKING FABRIC

The Backtack Technique

Because it calls for stapling fabric directly to walls, backtacking eliminates the need for panels and furring strips. An inherently simple technique, backtacking hides both fraying edges of material and staples by folding successive layers of fabric back over narrow strips of cardboard. You'll need upholsterer's tape, usually available as a continuous roll of narrow (less than ½ inch wide) cardboard stripping, a plumb line, long-nose pliers for removing poorly seated staples, and padding (¾-inch-thick bonded polyester batting is a convenient choice). An air-powered staple gun (be sure to read the pointers on the opposite page) and a friend's willing hands can also be big helps.

Padding. Staple batting to the wall in full-length strips from ceiling molding to baseboards. Don't worry about whether the edges of the batting and finish material coincide; there's little chance that spaces between the strips of padding will show. Working from a ladder or stool, first staple the top of the padding, then the upper left side. Pull the batting tight and staple the upper right side, then, stepping to the floor, continue down the sides. Staple across the bottom, tugging down until the material is taut. Trim the excess with knife or scissors.

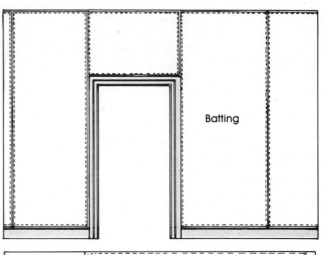

Batting

Cutting and ironing. Based on the calculations you made to purchase your fabric (see page 89), begin cutting the fabric into individual lengths, remembering to add the 2 inches of excess needed at the top and bottom of each strip. After every three or four strips, iron the panels and lay them out on a clean surface.

Stapling the first and second strips. Pick an inconspicuous spot—against a little-noticed corner or door frame, for example—and use just enough staples to hold the left edge of your first strip in place. Always staple as close to the edge of the fabric as possible while you hold the material tautly in place. Pull the fabric taut against the ceiling molding and staple at ½-inch to 3-inch intervals. Now go back and fill in the left side with similarly spaced staples. Switching to the right side, work your way from top to bottom, pulling the material taut as you go and stapling at 5-inch or 6-inch intervals. Go back to the top of the fabric and, again pulling the material tight as you work down the right side, fill in with closely spaced staples as before.

Drop a plumb line about ¾ inch inside the right edge of the first strip, against the fabric. Using the line as a guide, position the second strip wrong side out over the first, with its edge aligned with the plumb line. Baste-staple the wrong side of the second strip over the first strip in the upper left-hand corner and across the ceiling. Now line up the upholsterer's tape along the right edge and drive two or three staples through the top of the tape as well as the first and second strips. If necessary, pull out the staples with long-nose pliers and adjust the edge of the upholsterer's tape to make it even with the plumb line. Once the tape is properly aligned, secure with staples spaced from ½ inch to 3 inches apart.

With long-nose pliers, gently remove the basting staples. Pull the second strip straight across, back over and against the tape (now underneath the second strip's left edge). Follow the same procedure as with the first strip, stapling across the top, then down along the right edge, pulling the material taut as you go. Finish by stapling the material down at the baseboard. Continue

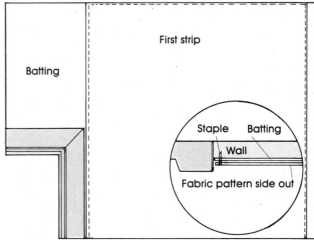

First strip

Batting

Staple   Batting

Wall

Fabric pattern side out

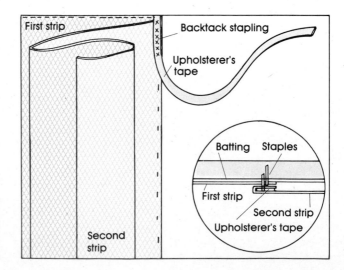

First strip

Backtack stapling

Upholsterer's tape

Batting   Staples

First strip

Second strip

Upholsterer's tape

Second strip

around the room, striking a plumb line at each strip's right edge, positioning the next strip wrong side out over its predecessor, then backtacking over the upholsterer's tape, and so on until finished.

Doors and windows. Cut separate pieces—they're known as headers and can be cut from scrap—to cover areas above and below windows and doors. Line the first header up with the right edge of the last full strip. Backtack, using a shortened length of upholsterer's tape equal to the height of the area you're covering—from door frame to ceiling, for example. Leave a margin of extra material—2 to 3 inches is enough—where fabric butts against door or window frame (so you can staple fabric as tightly into frame as possible).

Obstacles. Make your way around light fixtures and similar objects the same way you would with wallpaper

(see pages 82–83). Cut a hole in the batting and slip it under the base plate. When you apply the fabric, cut an *X* in it, pop the fixture through, and finish so that the base of the fixture is secured over the fabric. Be careful to keep fabric edges away from any bare wires.

Finishing touches. To bring the backtacking cycle to an end, slip-stitch the right edge of the last fabric strip to the left edge of the first strip you stapled. (You can't backtack because it's the final piece of fabric.) Since this seam will inevitably look a bit different from the others, plan your job so that it begins and ends at an inconspicuous place—against an unobtrusive door frame, perhaps. To hide stapled edges, finish with wood or metal molding strips, or use an electric glue gun, available at art supply stores, to attach braid or gimp. Touch up wrinkled spots with a hand steamer.

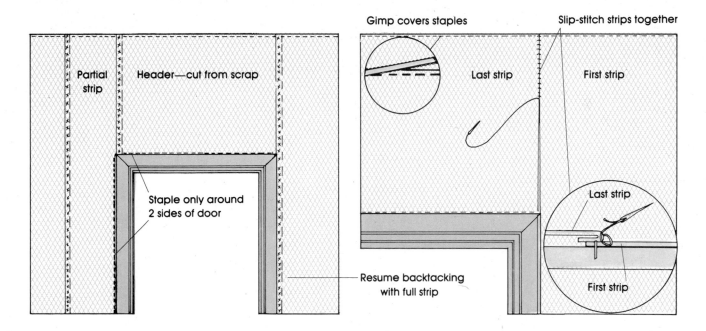

Partial strip

Header—cut from scrap

Staple only around 2 sides of door

Gimp covers staples

Slip-stitch strips together

Last strip

First strip

Last strip

First strip

Resume backtacking with full strip

Stapling Hints

Unless you're a professional or are blessed with exceptional strength, a room-size stapling project is going to leave you with some very sore muscles. An electric or air-powered staple gun can make it easier and help you do a better job in the bargain. When stapling, keep the following points in mind.

1. For full holding power, press the stapler flat against the material, and don't be afraid to use lots of staples.

2. To hold cloth in place temporarily, baste-staple by tilting the gun so the staple is only partially inserted.

3. Always try to drive staples parallel and as close as possible to moldings, baseboards, and fabric edges. This will permit you to use smaller, more delicate braid, gimp, rope, or molding to finish the project. Stapling at close intervals will also help you avoid baggy areas of material.

4. Be very careful when working with the stapler. Don't get your free hand in the way of the gun when stapling. If the gun jams, turn off the power and pump the trigger several times before trying to clear it. *Never pull the trigger on any stapler while it is pointed at your face or body.*

FABRIC ON RODS

Because it creates wallcoverings that are both inexpensive and highly portable, the technique of shirring material on rods can be especially appealing if you rent your home. Shirring can help hide severely cracked walls as well as add continuity to a room by extending color or a pattern from drapes or furniture to the walls. One especially attractive feature about shirring is that the fabric can easily be removed for washing or replacement.

Choosing Fabric

It's best to stick with lightweight materials—designer sheets, chintz, or sailcloth, for example—to help reduce weight on the rods, which typically are supported only at their ends. Small, nondirectional patterns are preferable to large designs. Its soft, delicate folds make shirring best suited for bedroom applications. If possible, try to find a helper before attempting the shirred fabric technique described here. As in many wallcovering jobs, four hands are often better than two.

Measuring Fabric

To calculate the yardage needed for a shirred wallcovering, start by using the process described for other fabric panels (see page 89). If the wall you are covering includes windows, doors, or other openings, treat the areas above and below the opening as separate rectangles, and add their fabric requirements to the remainder of the wall. When you get your total, triple it—shirring requires a lot of extra yardage to allow for gathering.

Cutting Fabric

Cut all the panels you intend to use, figuring on three strips of material for each single area of vertical and horizontal wall space (remember that you're tripling the amount of material you put on the walls). Add 10 to 14 inches to the vertical length of each panel to allow for top and bottom rod pockets (use the smaller figure for plain pockets, the larger for pockets with ruffles, as discussed at right).

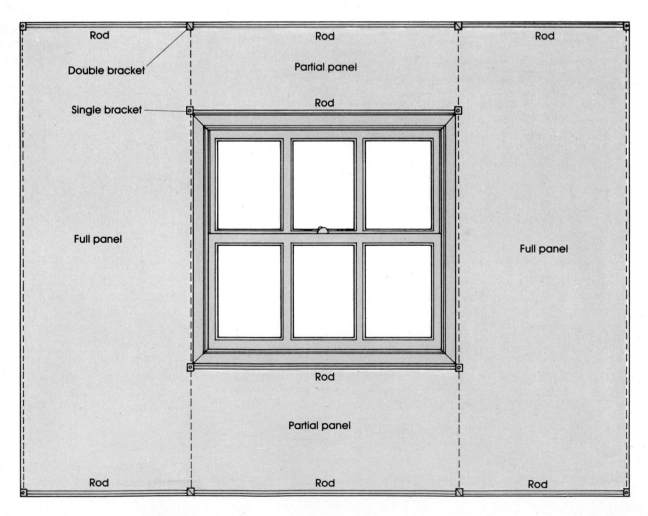

Sewing Fabric

Seam the strips of fabric into panels, being careful to match patterns. (Use a sewing machine—the quantity even in a small room is much too much for hand sewing.) Where it butts against doors or windows, fabric should be turned under and ironed flat.

You'll need to make rod pockets for both the top and the bottom edge. Do the top pocket first. For a plain rod pocket, fold about 1¾ inches of the fabric to the wrong side. Turn the raw edge under ½ inch and iron the pocket flat. Stitch across the entire width of the fabric just above the turned-under edge. For a ruffled pocket, turn to the wrong side about 3¾ inches of material and run two parallel lines of stitching, one across the bottom of the pocket and the other about 2 inches below the top fold. To ensure a proper fit, you may want to trial-hang the panel on your wall before sewing the bottom pocket.

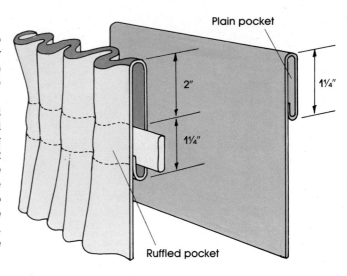

Plain pocket

2"

1¼"

1¼"

Ruffled pocket

Installing Shirred Fabric

Projecting decorative rods—polished brass, for example—are sometimes used when shirred fabric is intended to cover only a small portion of a wall. For most full-wall jobs, however, it's best to use flat curtain rods (i.e., without the bends used to hang fabric over doors and windows) and flush-to-the-wall curtain rod brackets. Use single brackets when the fabric is mounted straight across a plain wall and double brackets wherever an opening, such as a window, dictates that two rods meet.

Always install the top rod first. Mark the upper bracket mounting holes near the ceiling, allowing enough clearance (usually at least an inch) to rotate the rod onto the bracket. If your panels include a ruffle, allow enough additional vertical space to accommodate the ruffle without exposing the wall. The fabric should conceal the wall without crumpling against the ceiling. Using wood screws or expansion bolts, mount the brackets to support the rod at each end. Remove cover plates from electrical switches or outlets.

Place the rods in the pockets and mount the upper rod in its brackets, allowing the weight of the bottom rod to pull the fabric into place. Smooth the material with your hands. When the fabric hangs against the wall without excess tension or bagginess, mark appropriate holes for the bottom-rod mounting brackets and install the rod.

Pull the fabric tight around switches or outlets. Cut a rectangle in the fabric just a bit smaller than the box, so that the plate will cover fabric edges when it is replaced. To cover the plate, cut a fabric rectangle somewhat larger than the plate to allow for wraparound. Using paste or glue, apply the fabric to the plate, cutting away the corners and pressing fabric flat. Replace the cover plate, tightening it into position to hold the surrounding fabric in place.

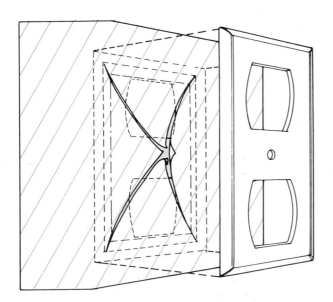

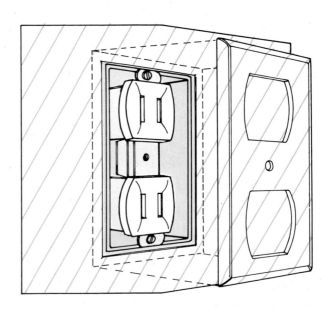

NATURAL WOOD FINISHES

As is the case when painting woodwork, staining and sealing are usually done last if you are painting the room and first if you are using a wallcovering. For new—that is, unfinished—wood, first stain, then seal. Previously finished trim needs only sealing. For better control, it's probably best to stick with single-purpose stains and varnishes. Stain should be applied with a clean piece of cheesecloth; a brush can leave puddles where it first touches the surface. Use natural-bristle brushes for sealing, 4 inches wide for doors and other broad surfaces, 2½ inches wide for frames and moldings. Buy the highest quality brush you can—it will pay off in fewer bristles to be picked off the surface before it dries. To avoid the risk of unwanted color creeping into your finish, don't apply a sealant with a brush that has previously been used to apply paint.

Staining

Stains can be used to change the color of wood, imparting to pine, for example, the mellowness of maple or the dark hues of walnut, or they can enrich the tones already present in a nice piece of wood. Use the manufacturer-supplied chip in selecting stain color, but always try out the stain on a piece of scrap wood to see the effect it creates before applying it to your trim.

Seal first. Wood often absorbs stain unevenly—soft, open grain soaks up more stain than dense grain does. For that reason, your first step in any stain job should be to brush or wipe on a coat of clear stain, sometimes called stain controller. When it's dry, sand with 220-grit paper. Then lightly dip cheesecloth into the colored stain and apply it to the trim. Most stains should be wiped off after they've penetrated the wood; consult the manufacturer's instructions for the recommended time between application and removal. For most jobs, figure on a minimum of two coats of stain, unless you're striving for a very light effect. The additional coats will give a richer appearance and add more depth to the finish. You can control the color best by applying a series of thin coats of stain rather than several heavy ones; thin coats will dry faster too. Keep in mind that varnish is likely to make your stain job look a little darker.

Getting an even color. If your wood absorbs the stain unevenly, or if you need to match different pieces of wood—for example, when a strip of darker wood has been used to repair an otherwise lighter baseboard—you may have to use more than one color of stain in order to obtain an even color. One often successful approach is first to stain only the light section, then cover the entire area with a second color until a uniform appearance is achieved.

Note: always wear rubber gloves when staining. Getting stain off your hands can be more difficult than getting it on the wood.

Sealing

After staining, most natural woodwork jobs call for one or more top coats of a clear finish. Nordic seamen used boiled linseed oil as a coating to protect their ships and longboats. More recently, shellac—made from the shells of small scale insects dissolved in alcohol—was popular as an interior wood finish. Shellac is fast-drying, but it is fragile and has a tendency to yellow in sunlight. It is also highly flammable; it should never be applied in the presence of open flame, including pilot lights. The directions below are for varnish, probably today's most widely used finish for interior woodwork. Urethane, essentially a liquid plastic, boasts greater durability, which makes it especially suited for floors, but it is more difficult to sand. A liquid drying agent, available from your paint dealer, may be added to either urethane or varnish to speed drying time.

Note: if you are using varnish that has been stored for a while, it may have "skinned over" in the can. If so, cut around the inside of the can with a fresh razor blade and carefully lift out the "skin." Then pour the varnish through a strainer before using.

1. Using your fingernail or a small penknife, flick or chip at existing varnish, removing loose pieces, until what's left seems solid, then feather the edges with medium-fine-grade sandpaper.

2. Wipe the sanded area with a tack cloth, stroking with the grain of the wood to remove all dust; any remaining particles will prevent the varnish from adhering.

3. Wearing rubber gloves, apply liquid deglossing agent to prepare the surface for varnishing. Use terrycloth—it will hold more of the fast-evaporating liquid—and follow the contours of the wood. When you are finished, thoroughly rinse all used rags in water, then dispose of them in a closed container away from heat or flame.

4. Apply petroleum jelly with a small, stiff-bristled brush to hinges or other hardware you don't want to varnish.

5. For your first finish coat, pour a small amount of varnish into a coffee can and cut 25 percent with thinner. (This will help varnish penetrate the wood and reduce the number of brush marks.) Brush the thinned varnish over the surface to be finished.

6. Allow varnish to dry. Sand, using 220-grit paper or fine steel wool. Apply a coat of full-strength varnish. Recoat as necessary, sanding before each coat; two to three coats should be sufficient for previously finished surfaces, but new wood will probably require three to five. If the final coat seems too glossy, buff lightly with fine steel wool.

Cleanup note: be sure to clean brushes thoroughly between coats or tiny clumps of varnish may be deposited in subsequent coats.

U.S. Measure and Metric Measure Conversion Chart

		Formulas for Exact Measure			Rounded Measures for Quick Reference			
	Symbol	When you know:	Multiply by:	To find:				
Mass (Weight)	oz	ounces	28.35	grams	1 oz			= 30 g
	lb	pounds	0.45	kilograms	4 oz			= 115 g
	g	grams	0.035	ounces	8 oz			= 225 g
	kg	kilograms	2.2	pounds	16 oz	=	1 lb	= 450 g
					32 oz	=	2 lb	= 900 g
					36 oz	=	2-1/4 lb	= 1000 g (1 kg)
Volume	tsp	teaspoons	5	milliliters	1/4 tsp	=	1/24 oz	= 1 ml
	tbsp	tablespoons	15	milliliters	1/2 tsp	=	1/12 oz	= 2 ml
	fl oz	fluid ounces	29.57	milliliters	1 tsp	=	1/6 oz	= 5 ml
	c	cups	0.24	liters	1 tbsp	=	1/2 oz	= 15 ml
	pt	pints	0.47	liters	1 c	=	8 oz	= 250 ml
	qt	quarts	0.95	liters	2 c (1 pt)	=	16 oz	= 500 ml
	gal	gallons	3.785	liters	4 c (1 qt)	=	32 oz	= 1 l
	ml	milliliters	0.034	fluid ounces	4 qt (1 gal)	=	128 oz	= 3-3/4 l
Length	in.	inches	2.54	centimeters	3/8 in.	=		1 cm
	ft	feet	30.48	centimeters	1 in.	=		2.5 cm
	yd	yards	0.9144	meters	2 in.	=		5 cm
	mi	miles	1.609	kilometers	2-1/2 in.	=		6.5 cm
	km	kilometers	0.621	miles	12 in. (1 ft)	=		30 cm
	m	meters	1.094	yards	1 yd	=		90 cm
	cm	centimeters	0.39	inches	100 ft	=		30 m
					1 mi	=		1.6 km
Temperature	F°	Fahrenheit	5/9 (after subtracting 32)	Celsius	32°F	=		0°C
					68°F	=		20°C
	C°	Celsius	9/5 +32	Fahrenheit	212°F	=		100°C
Area	in.²	square inches	6.452	square centimeters	1 in.²	=		6.5 cm²
	ft²	square feet	929	square centimeters	1 ft²	=		930 cm²
	yd²	square yards	8361	square centimeters	1 yd²	=		8360 cm²
	a	acres	.4047	hectares	1 a	=		4050 m²

Index